THE FALCON METHOD

THE
FALCON
METHOD

*A Proven System for Building
Passive Income and Wealth
Through Stock Investing*

DAVID SOLYOMI

ISBN: 978-1-63161-040-0

Published by TCK Publishing

www.TCKPublishing.com

Get discounts and special deals on our bestselling books at

www.tckpublishing.com/bookdeals

Contents

Why This Book?

If you are like me, you have probably run across several trading and investment approaches that promised to make you rich but failed to live up to those expectations. But within just a few pages, you'll realize that this book and the FALCON Method it describes are completely different and can truly set you on the path to becoming a successful long-term investor regardless of your current experience level. After years of learning from hundreds of investment books and my own mistakes, I find myself wishing I'd had the chance to read such a concise summary of all the important aspects of investing wisely before I had set sail into money management.

No matter how you ended up here, this book will show you:

- Why you absolutely must invest in stocks if you are aiming to build wealth and a predictable passive income stream.

- How you should reduce the universe of stocks from tens of thousands of possibilities to a few hundred candidates that have the characteristics that are proven to drive superior performance.

- How to tell which of these top-quality stocks are available on the cheap, thus offering a turbo-boost to your returns (AKA the double-dip benefit).

- What absolute threshold criteria you should set before putting your money into any investment.

- How to rank the stocks that seem to have it all: both top quality and attractive valuation.

- What other aspects to examine before committing your capital to a promising investment candidate.

- And last but not least: how to make the most of an investment approach—the FALCON Method—that gives you a list of the best stocks every month. Knowing the names of the Top10 stocks is not everything, believe me!

Successful investing requires structured decision-making based on a well-built process—and this is exactly what you will learn in this book. In fact, you can get a glimpse of the FALCON Method flowchart after the Foreword and see for yourself what steps it utilizes to achieve superior performance. (In the following chapters, you will get to know all of them one by one.)

I want to emphasize that I am the type of guy who is most definitely putting his money where his mouth is, so **I am managing my own investments based on the approach covered in this book, following the exact same process**. In fact, I have built the FALCON Method from scratch—it took years of gradual improvements and fine-tuning to reach the standard you are about to learn here. As a wonderful side effect, I achieved financial freedom along the way at the age of just 33, proving that this process really works!

You can get to know my personal story in detail in the About the Author chapter, which was confined to the end of the book. At this point, suffice it to say that I've established and sold some companies, so I gathered plenty of experience as both a corporate insider and an outside investor. I completely agree with Warren Buffett that being a businessman does help one to become a better investor and vice versa.

After surrendering all my executive roles, I became a full-time investor. **I wrote a best-selling book on dividend investing in Hungary**, where I live, and shared my knowledge in both personal and online training formats while also taking up speaking engagements at financial conferences. I enjoy what I am doing—

investing is my passion and this will show through on the following pages, where I have spiced up the useful content with a little bit of humor to make your learning adventure fun and easy.

Don't fear—investment doesn't have to be daunting. You will surely be able to grasp and use what I am about to share with you because I packaged it into a simple and easy-to-digest format. I'm not the kind of person who uses jargon just to showcase his financial education. And because I'm already living off passive income, I am not even writing this book with a definite financial motivation or in search of sales—instead, I wrote it to help you start along the same path that made achieving my childhood dreams possible. You don't even need to become a full-time investor like me—**a few hours per month should be more than enough to profit immensely from what you will learn here**.

Let me walk you through all you should know to get outstanding results as a long-term investor, using 100% honesty and a little bit of humor so that we both enjoy the journey. And before we move on, as an extra guarantee for your time invested, I am offering you my personal help when you start out as an investor. Now you have plenty of reasons to read on!

PREFACE

What Makes a Good Company and a Good Investment?

The value of an investment is determined by the amount of cash it can pay you, the timing and probability of these payments, and the prevailing risk-free interest rate. If this sounds complex, it's not, really: let me show you how sensible investing can be simple and rewarding at the same time.

History shows us that stocks provide the best returns in the long run. Since stocks are not lottery tickets but rather represent ownership stakes in real companies, there are just two questions a successful investor must be able to answer:

WHAT MAKES A GOOD COMPANY?

A firm that produces more cash than it consumes and only needs to retain a fraction of this surplus cash to maintain the standard of its operations and its competitiveness can be a promising candidate for investment. The key is having this "no-strings-attached cash," which can either serve as the source of further growth or can be returned to the owners.

OPERATIONS

To understand the importance of this "no-strings-attached cash," think about a company that needs to invest all the cash it makes just to stay competitive and be able to make the exact same amount of cash the next year—which, of course, needs to be retained again just for the sake of survival. As an owner of this company, your chances of receiving cash back from your investment are very slim; this alone renders such a company an unattractive target for investment.

The essence of a company's operations can be grasped by following the "no-strings-attached cash" it generates and the return it makes on the capital employed. The company's management must be capable of achieving a rate of return on the company's invested capital that is superior to what you could get as a private investor. Otherwise, why keep your money in the firm? This both sounds simple and is fairly straightforward to gauge, too.

So a good company produces tons of surplus cash and earns high rates of return on its invested capital. It's a great thing if the corporate operations look splendid, but all that glitters is not gold. Making loads of cash is just one part of the story—what the management does with this money is equally important.

This is where capital allocation skills come into play. You want to be the owner of a company that not only makes a huge amount of the attractive "no-strings-attached cash" category, but uses it wisely as well…and treats its shareholders fairly, too. Otherwise, it would be like printing cash in one room just to burn it in another.

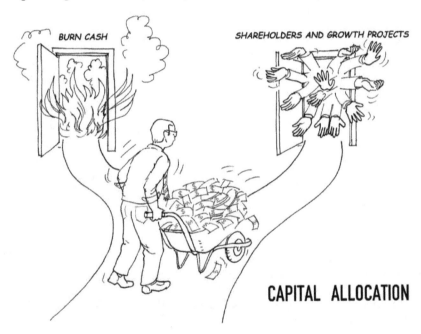

BURN CASH

SHAREHOLDERS AND GROWTH PROJECTS

CAPITAL ALLOCATION

WHAT MAKES A GOOD INVESTMENT?

As we've seen, a good company excels in the operations and capital allocation dimensions. But these alone will not make it a good investment, since the company will give you subpar returns if you overpay for the shares. This is where the third key dimension, valuation, comes into play. You need to buy stocks of quality companies when they are available on the cheap—that's the recipe for stock market success and wealth building. As obvious as it sounds, this has been proven to work for centuries, as we will soon see.

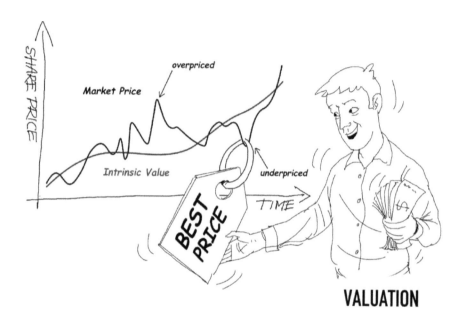

YOU EITHER HAVE A PROCESS OR YOU ARE JUST GAMBLING

> *"When somebody calls, I can usually tell within two or three minutes whether a deal is likely to happen or not. There are just half a dozen filters, and it either makes through the filters or not."*
> ~ Warren Buffett in a Bloomberg video interview, 2016[1]

Identifying the quality stocks that are on sale can be easy if you have a well-built process to help you. It is like having a machine with an input slot and an output slot: 300 stocks go in and the 10 best come out. This is exactly what the FALCON Method is doing, relying on the principles of value investing, common sense, and quantitative discipline.

PROCESS VS. GAMBLING

You can get a grasp of the underlying process by studying the flowchart in the following chapter. However, to gain a really good understanding, you should read the entire book. By the end, you will have become a better investor. Then you have a choice: I can help you implement what you have learned or you can continue your journey alone.

No matter which route you choose, you will benefit immensely from learning the all-round investment approach of the FALCON Method.

FLOWCHART OF THE FALCON METHOD

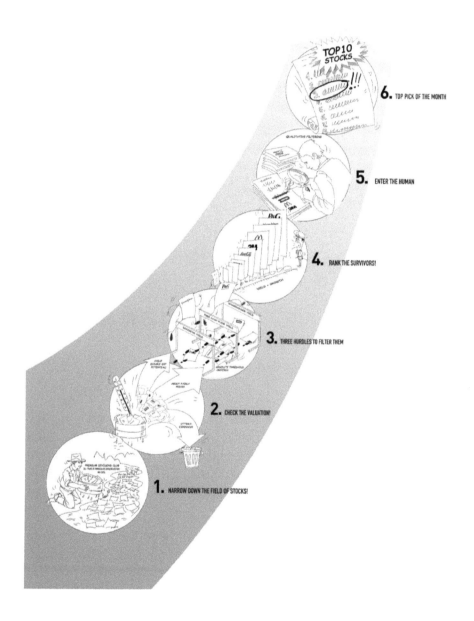

1

The True Story Behind the FALCON Method

L et me prepare you for the honesty you will encounter in this book with a short story. Any marketing guy would advise against admitting the true origin of the system's name, but I will go with my gut and share the real behind-the-scenes story.

Tons of fake origin stories could be fabricated, listing similarities between the falcon and a good investor. Here are a few, just for pure entertainment:

- Nothing can hide from the eyes of the falcon. Wikipedia says: "As is the case with many birds of prey, falcons have exceptional powers of vision; the visual acuity of one species has been measured at 2.6 times that of a normal human." How profitable could it be if an investor noticed opportunities that others miss, while objectively scanning the field of targets from the distance without any emotional biases? But come on, this has nothing to do with the origin of the name, however convincing it may sound!

- Falcons never hesitate; whenever they see a delicious bite, they go for it. And fast! "Peregrine falcons have been recorded diving at speeds of 200 miles per hour (320 km/h), making them the fastest-moving creatures on Earth." This was from Wikipedia again, as I hardly know anything about falcons myself. Once again, this was absolutely not the reason for picking the name FALCON Method.

- Falcons have exceptional hunting skills… Well, instead of elaborating on this obvious parallelism, I feel it is time for my confession.

In 2016, I had a meeting with a person who was, in fact, a marketing guy. He offered me his opinion about how I could reach a wider audience with my best-selling Hungarian book on dividend investing and its related online courses. At one point, he just stared at me and out of the blue, said: "You should write your book and create your courses in English, but as there are thousands of books on dividend investing on Amazon, you need a brand to stand out from the crowd. I would call it the FALCON Method or something like that."

Well, my family name means "falcon" if translated to English, but I honestly do not know how this idea came to him. As ridiculous as it sounded, I simply ignored his comment. I created a short video course in English, but of course didn't brand it the "FALCON Method." While that course was available on popular e-learning platforms, I registered the domain of my name (davidsolyomi.com) and started experimenting with building a WordPress site without any specific purpose. I named one of the menus "The FALCON Method" and created a dropdown menu with two options: "FREE videos" and "FULL video training." (This was the biggest achievement of my site-building career.)

As I gained hundreds of students on the e-learning platforms and my dividend investing course became a bestseller, strange emails started to flow in. It seemed that after watching my videos, people were Googling my name and found that the site was "under construction," to put it mildly. They started to contact me, asking questions about where the FALCON Method mentioned on the site was available because they most definitely wanted to purchase it.

I had a good laugh when reading the first such email. The second one made me think a little bit, while the third one almost made me admit that the marketing guy might be a true genius. (I would never, ever tell him that, so I hope he is not reading this!) And as these emails continued, I strongly felt that I should not hold the falcon captive any longer: I should let it fly if the demand was that high.

This is the true reason for choosing the name FALCON Method for the most all-round investment approach I am aware of and that you are about to learn in the following pages. I hope you'll enjoy this same kind of honesty and a bit of humor throughout the book, because I believe it'll make our journey together more useful and fun.

Why Stocks? (For The Long Run)

*"Investing is forgoing consumption now in order to have the
ability to consume more at a later date."*
~ Warren Buffett, 2011

Before getting into the details of stock selection and showing you how my system works, I want you to be 100% convinced that stocks are the absolute best asset class to invest in if you are aiming to build wealth and generate reliable income in the long term.

Having experienced violent swings in the stock market myself, I am sure that understanding the investment concept you are about to employ and being totally committed to following it is crucial; it will serve as the basis of outstanding results. Without this part, you are likely to give up executing the strategy at the worst possible moment, doing serious harm to your financial future.

So, let's lay down those basics as quickly and effectively as possible.

Warren Buffett, one of the world's most successful investors, draws up three major investment categories in his 2011Letter to Shareholders:[2]

> *"Investment possibilities are both many and varied. There are three major categories, however, and it's important to understand the characteristics of each.*
>
> *1. Investments that are denominated in a given currency include money-market funds, bonds, mortgages, bank deposits, and other instruments. Most of these currency-based investments are thought of as 'safe.' In truth, they are among the most dangerous of assets. Over the past century, these instruments have destroyed the purchasing power of investors in many countries, even as the holders continued to receive timely payments of interest and principal. This ugly result, moreover, will forever recur. Governments determine the ultimate value of money, and systemic forces will sometimes cause them to gravitate to policies that produce inflation. Current rates, however, do not come close to offsetting the purchasing-power risk that investors assume. Right now, bonds should come with a warning label. Today, a wry comment that Wall Streeter Shelby Cullom Davis made long ago seems apt: 'Bonds promoted as offering risk-free returns are now priced to deliver return-free risk.'"*

To sum up, the first category of fixed-income type investments gives you just what it advertises: a fixed income component. The problem is, nobody knows what that future sum (interests and the return of your principal) will be worth at the time you're entitled to get it. By investing in fixed-income products, you are basically speculating on the future rate of inflation, and such macroeconomic speculation seldom turns out to be successful[3]. With some investments in this first category, you can spare yourself the agony of price fluctuations (AKA volatility), although in return for the tranquility, you will slowly but surely lose your purchasing power[4]. Assuming this is not your goal, let's move on!

> *"2. The second major category of investments involves assets that will never produce anything, but that are purchased in the*

buyer's hope that someone else—who also knows that the assets will be forever unproductive—will pay more for them in the future.

Owners are not inspired by what the asset itself can produce— it will remain lifeless forever—but rather by the belief that others will desire it even more avidly in the future."

This second category is all about speculation and has nothing to do with investing. Buffett brings up the example of gold, which never produces anything, so anyone purchasing it is basically hoping that someday fear will motivate a larger group of people to buy gold, thus driving up its price. If you are buying unproductive assets, you are waiting for a bigger fool to come along and pay more for them than you did—and if that person fails to show up, *you* are the one left holding the bag. Speculation is not something you should build your financial future on.

Assuming you agree, let's see what Warren Buffett advocates! His reasoning is crystal clear, as usual.

"3. My own preference—and you knew this was coming—is our third category: investment in productive assets, whether businesses, farms, or real estate. Ideally, these assets should have the ability in inflationary times to deliver output that will retain its purchasing-power value while requiring a minimum of new capital investment.

Whether the currency a century from now is based on gold, seashells, shark teeth, or a piece of paper (as today), people will be willing to exchange a couple of minutes of their daily labor for a Coca-Cola

Our country's businesses will continue to efficiently deliver goods and services wanted by our citizens. Metaphorically, these commercial "cows" will live for centuries and give ever greater quantities of "milk" to boot. Their value will be determined not by the medium of exchange but rather by their capacity to deliver milk.

I believe that over any extended period of time, this category of investing will prove to be the runaway winner among the three we've examined. More important, it will be by far the safest."

What shall I add? Buffett is right: investing in productive assets like buying partial ownership stakes in quality companies in the form of shares is the "runaway winner" in the long run. Before I call on Professor Jeremy Siegel[5] from Wharton to back up Buffett's statements with some data, I feel I need to clear up the meaning of the last sentence in the above quotation. By calling them "the safest," Warren Buffett means that the assets within this third category have the greatest probability of preserving and growing your purchasing power. **Risk is the probability of permanent capital loss and has nothing to do with the price fluctuations of various investments.** This is where most people go wrong: they chase bonds because of their illusory safety (low volatility) while avoiding stocks because their prices fluctuate. That's the opposite of what you should be doing, though!

Let's see why you shouldn't fear stocks and why you absolutely must invest in them if you are gunning for the best financial future possible.

> *"How many millionaires do you know who have become wealthy by investing in savings accounts?"*
>
> ~ Robert G. Allen[6]

Professor Siegel's widely referenced book, *Stocks for the Long Run*, contains an invaluable set of data to draw conclusions from. In the fifth edition, he examined asset returns from 1802 to 2012 and compiled the chart below to showcase his findings.

FIGURE 1-1

Total Real Returns on U.S. Stocks, Bonds, Bills, Gold, and the Dollar, 1802–2012

Asset Class	Annualized Return
Stocks	6.6%
Bonds	3.6%
Bills	2.7%
Gold	0.7%
US Dollar	-1.4%

These are real returns, reflecting the effect of inflation and showing how your future purchasing power could vary based on the investment asset you pick. Stocks are way off the chart, while hoarding cash is the worst possible thing you can do.(Note that investing $1 in the stock market multiplied your purchasing power by almost 705,000 between 1802 and 2012, while the second best asset only had a multiple of 1,778. A huge gap indeed!)

> *"By a continuing process of inflation, governments can confiscate, secretly and unobserved, an important part of the wealth of their citizens.*
>
> *The process engages all the hidden forces of economic law on the side of destruction, and does it in a manner which not one man in a million is able to diagnose."*
>
> ~ John Maynard Keynes[7]

Are you serious about building wealth? Stocks are the vehicle you need to use, as centuries of data and the insights from the most reputable and accomplished investors in the world show. Accepting this fact is the first crucial step toward success.

Now let's move on and clear up the mystery that surrounds stocks and the stock market!

3

The Black Box

"Stocks aren't lottery tickets. There's a company attached to every share."

~ Peter Lynch[8]

There is nothing special or hard to understand about stocks. A stock simply represents an ownership stake in a company. If you buy a share of Coca-Cola, you become an owner of that company and are entitled to your share of profits. It is as simple as that— although the financial industry doesn't want you to get the picture and have the courage to invest on your own, so they deliberately try to overcomplicate things and use jargon most people don't understand. After all, they have to make money somehow, even if they provide a shocking disservice by not being able to invest better than you could, despite still offering their "help" at a really hefty price[9].

At this point, you must be convinced that you should invest in stocks. You know that with stocks, you are basically investing in the underlying companies. Now it's time to take a look at how a company operates and how it can generate and use cash, since understanding this will be the key to your financial future. (Don't be afraid! The solution I draw up with the FALCON Method will free you from analyzing all the factors one by one, but I still feel you should have a look at them once to get a better understanding of how everything works under the hood.)

I came across a very illustrative description of how a company operates in David van Knapp's book *Sensible Stock Investing*[10], so I will use his model to highlight all the points that are good to know. The following picture will simplify things:

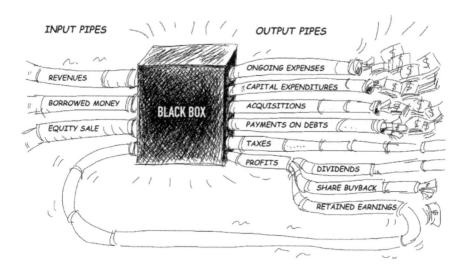

First of all, when thinking about a company financially, consider it to be a black box. You must accept that because you're an outsider, you have absolutely no chance to know with any certainty what is happening inside that black box. The good news is that you do not actually *need* this knowledge to create a reliable and growing passive income and achieve outstanding total returns from your investments. Since a company is all about value creation, meaning that it must generate more money than the amount that went in, you will be perfectly fine focusing on the money pipes connected to the black box. Let's see what input pipes can carry money into the box!

The input pipes are:

- Revenues: The money the company receives from customers of its products and services.
- Borrowed money: The firm can get a bank loan or issue bonds to finance its operations. The key will be how the management puts this borrowed money to use and what return it can squeeze out of it.*(Hint: it should be way above the interest paid.)*
- Equity sale: The company can issue new shares, thus diluting its existing shareholders' stakes. It is extremely important to have a look at this input pipe, because many companies are funding their dividend payments from this source—which is not desirable, to put it mildly. (Too many dividend investors don't pay attention to this and can fall prey to unfair practices employed by a company's management.)

"Other companies sell newly issued shares to Peter in order to pay dividends to Paul. Beware of dividends that can be paid out only if someone promises to replace the capital distributed."

~ Warren Buffett, 1981[11]

The output pipes are the following:

- Ongoing expenses: These are about financing the company's day-to-day operations. This pipe typically includes salaries, office supplies, marketing and advertising costs, etc.
- Capital expenditures: This is money spent on things that have a useful life of more than one year, like computers, machinery, buildings, etc.
- Acquisitions of other companies: One form of growth can be the purchase of other companies.
- Payments on debts: The money that the "borrowed money" income pipe brought into the black box does not come for free.

This output pipe shows how much the company pays out to service its debt.

- Taxes: This is pretty self-explanatory. All companies have to pay their fair share to the government.

- Profits: Intelligent investors keep close tabs on not only the level of profits a company makes but also the way it uses the surplus cash it generates[12]. The dimension of capital allocation is just as important as profit generation.

> *"We, as well as many other businesses, are likely to retain earnings over the next decade that will equal, or even exceed, the capital we presently employ. Some companies will turn these retained dollars into fifty-cent pieces, others into two-dollar bills.*
>
> *This 'what-will-they-do-with-the-money' factor must always be evaluated along with the 'what-do-we-have-now' calculation in order for us, or anybody, to arrive at a sensible estimate of a company's intrinsic value."*
>
> ~ Warren Buffett, 2010[13]

Paying attention to Buffett's words, investors should focus on what a company's profits are used for. In the FALCON Method, we surely will! But to get you ready to tackle this key component, let's have a look at **the three possible uses of profits**: the sub-pipes of the "Profits" pipe!

- Dividends: The company can pay part of its profits to its shareholders. *(Hint: You will love the money flowing through this pipe!)*

- Share buyback: When a company spends a certain part of its surplus cash to purchase its (hopefully undervalued) shares on the open market, it can decrease the total number of shares that represent the underlying company. As a result of the decreasing share count, the earnings per share figure grows. To paraphrase the title of a bestselling book: there are at least "50 shades" of buybacks, so we will pay attention to this pipe along with share issuances in order to help us identify value creation and destruction.

- Retained earnings: Through this pipe, the company recycles money back into itself for growth and expansion, so this becomes the fourth input pipe. Again, the key here will be how efficiently the management can employ this capital.

This is all you need to know to understand how to pick the right companies to invest in—and this was the toughest part of the book, I promise! You will not need to learn this model by heart, but it is useful to read it through so that you can gain a better understanding of why the FALCON Method is built the way it is. You may notice that the investment process I outline below really takes all the important variables into account and is much more than an oversimplified dividend investing model, of which you can find dozens, if not hundreds, on the market…most of them with serious flaws. (So serious, in fact, that after reading just these few brief pages, you'll be able to uncover some of them!)

To summarize: As an outsider, you should accept that the inner processes of a company will be hidden from you. Treat the company as a black box and focus on the input and output pipes that are attached to it! After all, corporate operations are about value creation: generating more money than the company uses in the process. You can grasp this perfectly by turning your attention to the pipes transferring the money. Don't take your eyes off the ball… I mean, money, and you will be fine!

It's somewhat sad to say, but even if this was your first reading about how a company operates, you already have a more nuanced understanding of the issue than most investors do.

One more thing before we move on: rest assured that you will not need to analyze these pipes that I have detailed one by one! The steps of the FALCON Method cover all the critical parts.

Now that you've learned the basics here, the rest of this book will be so logical and self-explanatory that you won't understand why you aren't already practicing the ideas I outline!

So let's see what purposes the FALCON Method serves, and set our goals properly before we get into the step-by-step process of implementation!

4

The Goal of the FALCON Method

"All the real money in investment will have to be made—as most of it has been in the past—not out of buying and selling but out of owning and holding securities, receiving interests and dividends therein, and benefiting from their long-term increases in value."

~ Benjamin Graham[14]

IT'S ALL ABOUT BUY AND HOLD! THIS IS NOT THE CLASSIC QUANT MODEL

The FALCON Method is meant to assist you in constructing a "buy and hold" stock portfolio. This is a far more important distinction than you may think. The classic and popular quant models are back-tested with the assumption that you are ranking stocks based on some quantitative criteria and then buying the best of them (the ones that ranked highest). You are supposed to hold these picks for 12 months, then sell them and repeat the process: do the ranking again and simply buy the stocks that rank highest at that time[15]. Quant investing means 100% mechanical investing.

Although there are some quantitative factors that are proven to explain outperformance, there are serious problems with the practical application of the classic quant approach.

First of all, most of these rankings produce a list of stocks featuring totally unknown companies that are very hard, if not impossible, for most investors to buy from a psychological perspective. (Would you commit your capital—your hard-earned cash—to something you'd never heard about? Most of us feel quite uncomfortable with this.)

The annual rebalancing of the portfolio is another issue. Back-tests seldom, if ever, factor in the transaction costs and tax effects of changing all the stocks in your portfolio every year. Plus, this practice doesn't come naturally for most investors. Still, if you sign up for the convincing promises of a quant model, you should follow its implementation to the letter, however bad it feels. (Otherwise, you may base your expectations on data that are not relevant for your modified investment process.)

> *"A portfolio is like a bar of soap: the more you handle it, the smaller it gets."*
> ~ Unknown

The most important shortcoming, however, is that no quant model performs exceptionally well every single year, so you will have to deal with bad results along the way, all while not being totally comfortable with the background of your stock selection. (Whichever quant strategy you choose, I bet you won't feel good about the "black box background" of the ranking process and the list of stocks it makes you purchase.) Understanding the logic of the strategy you are implementing and completely trusting the approach you're using are crucial to your future success, since you will have to stay the course in tough times as well as good.

> *"[Investing in quant models is] hard for people to do, for two main reasons. First, the companies that show up on the screens can be scary and not doing so well, so people find them difficult to buy. Second, there can be one-, two- or three-year periods when a strategy doesn't work.*

Most people aren't capable of sticking it out through that."
~ Joel Greenblatt[16]

Long story short: when investing, you will probably quickly give up using the classic quant models for psychological reasons, while you will be capable of sticking with the buy and hold approach of the FALCON Method. That's because you'll understand the process, and the stocks it suggests are mostly household names. It is easier psychologically to hold stocks in reputable, well-known companies that are putting more and more money into your pocket in the form of dividends than it is to buy stocks in unknown small companies and then change all of them when the year ends.

Active stock trading—buying and selling stocks often—is also a field that makes only a small proportion of adventurers rich. The reasons are numerous: psychological factors, transaction costs, and taxes, just to name a few.

Buy and hold is the way to go, and gives the best results for most investors.

MORE THAN JUST DIVIDENDS

The FALCON Method does not employ a pure income-focused strategy. There is much more to stock investing than the current dividend yield! Although our process embraces a wider scale of factors than most dividend investors do, we still get the predictable and growing passive income component by investing in companies that have been paying stable or increasing dividends for decades.

"Do you know the only thing that gives me pleasure? It's to see my dividends coming in."
~ John D. Rockefeller[17]

Besides focusing on dividends as an important part of our total return, the FALCON Method picks the list of stocks that are both producing the passive income we love and are available at bargain prices (that is, they are valued lower than their average historical valuation level). When the natural process of mean reversion comes into play and the valuation multiple expands, our total return gets a huge extra boost. (I will explain this in more detail later, illustrating the point with examples.)

In the end, by understanding that a stock's current dividend yield is only a part of the total return equation, you get much more than just a reliable and growing passive income. And you get more than just dividends, since you will be investing in a more sensible way than 95% of the people out there trying their luck with stocks.

By the end of this book, you will see that on the one hand, dividends are a very important factor in determining your total return, while on the other hand, **stable and growing dividends are the *symptom* of a wonderful corporate operation and by no means the cause of it**. Anyway, we are more than happy if such a symptom serves as a telltale sign for us to identify top-quality companies that have been generating more and more surplus cash for decades and rewarding their shareholders fairly along the way.

WITHOUT A SYSTEM, YOU ARE JUST GAMBLING

> *"The rational man—like the Loch Ness monster—is sighted often, but photographed rarely."*
> ~ David Dreman[18]

Most mistakes in investing come from psychological biases. Just imagine what irrational decision makers we must be when a whole new field of science called behavioral finance is flourishing these days! None of us can escape the biases we are born with—this is why we need to tackle those mental hangups in the best possible way, getting past them so we can make smarter choices.

I believe in structured decision-making and the consistent application of a logically built, proven system. This way, you can tilt the odds of success in your favor before your ego comes into play. Going by your instincts or investing without a system is all about dumb luck and can promise no consistent results. Focus on what you can control (the process) and the results will take care of themselves!

Do you happen to know why so few professional investors manage to beat the S&P 500 index in the long run? Because the index is totally emotion-free; it just consistently executes a very simple strategy (like investing in the 500 largest companies) without overthinking or changing its style, whereas most investors are not capable of staying the course and sticking with their chosen strategy in the long run. James O'Shaughnessy points this out in his wonderful book *What Works on Wall Street*.

The FALCON Method is built to limit psychological errors and emotional decision making. It's based on a well-structured process that only leaves room for subjectivity in the later phases, when it is already too late to make any costly mistakes, since basically all stocks that survive the filtering process until that last round provide significantly above-average investment opportunities.

Although my ego may feed on the belief that I can add extra value by carrying out some qualitative analysis at this last stage, this is hard to test (lucky me!), so I would rather overweight the proven factors of outperformance that are to be detailed on the following pages.

In summary: The FALCON Method is a structured stock selection process that helps to construct a buy and hold portfolio with a focus on both income and total return. The model is about 90% quantitative and 10% qualitative.

PUTTING ALL THESE INTO PRACTICE

"In theory, there is no difference between theory and practice.
In practice, there is."

~ Yogi Berra[19]

Anybody can fill pages with empty sentences about how to invest wisely and what you need to know to succeed. The difference is in how these lines are implemented after the talking is done.

1. First and foremost, because buy and hold is the best possible investment approach you can practice, we need to focus on a select group of stocks that are suitable for this strategy. These are reputable companies that have been making increasing

profits and paying growing dividends for decades. Such pre-filtering of the whole stock universe is absolutely necessary to help you stay the course in the long run.

2. The FALCON Method will never "sell" you the so-called "deep value trash" stocks that are cheap if evaluated on certain metrics but otherwise represent terrible companies. Such a quantitative approach can be rewarding for a small minority of people who are psychologically prepared to practice it—but when taking taxes and transaction costs into account, I am not sure that such strategies could significantly outperform the quality-focused buy and hold approach in the long run.

3. I advocate a SWAN (Sleep Well At Night) style of investing, since you only live once, and if your investments keep you up at night, you have basically ruined your life. This is too high a price for any return! If you were able to calculate some totally subjective indicator of returns that also took your feelings into account, I'm pretty sure that the investment approach you're learning here would rank highest.

4. Since you need to stay the course through thick and thin, dividends play an important part in our model. It is always easier to hold onto (and maybe even buy more of) the stocks of well-known companies that are paying you growing dividends, even when the stock market collapses, than to commit yourself to some microcap[20] garbage that's been spit out by a semi-reliable stock screener.

5. The power of understanding how the FALCON Method works cannot be overemphasized. **You should never blindly follow anyone who advertises himself as an extraordinary investor, because this is a sure path to huge losses.** I'm not the type of guy who will hard-sell you anything, be it a single stock pick or my investment newsletter. I believe in passing on valuable knowledge so that people can have an insight into what I am doing and why. This way, you can learn and prosper at the same time, while becoming a much better investor than you may be today.

6. Strong long-term performance always stems from staying the course. Remember the eye-opening example of the S&P 500 index? Consistency pays dividends! All of the previous points are there to help you stay the course and tilt the odds in your favor.

If you are dedicated to long-term wealth building and the thoughts above are resonating with your core values, then it's worth reading on and getting to know the components of the FALCON Method.

Outlining the Process of the FALCON Method

"Investing money is the process of committing resources in a strategic way to accomplish a specific objective."
~ Alan Gotthardt[21]

Next, you will learn about the components of the FALCON Method, but it's a good idea to take a look at the full picture before zooming in on its components one by one. So here's a brief summary:

1. Determine the group of stocks that are suitable for selection. *(Hint: we will be very picky, and for good reasons!)*

2. Which stocks on our list are available on the cheap side of their historical valuation levels? (I promised examples of an extra return boost; this is the section where you will find it.)

3. Which of the qualifying stocks fulfill our threshold criteria for capital allocation? If these absolute levels are not met, it is

simply not worth investing our money. Hold cash in the rare instances when nothing appears appetizing!

4. Rank the stocks that survived the first three steps! The FALCON Method employs a multifactor quantitative ranking that results in a list of the "crème de la crème."

5. Use a qualitative analysis to eliminate the stocks on the shortlist that I would not be comfortable investing in based on the synthesized knowledge derived from reading hundreds of investment books over the years. (Again: it is almost impossible to prove that this phase adds value to the process, but at least it makes me more comfortable investing in the final list of stocks. The power of this personal feeling is not to be underestimated, since a good investor has to stay the course in the periods of panic as well as plenty, and feeling comfortable with the stocks in your portfolio surely helps with that.)

By applying these steps, the FALCON Method gives you a list of the Top10 stocks that offer the best relative opportunities in the current market environment. Beyond this, I also highlight my Top Pick for the month: the stock I myself would go for at the moment.

A later chapter will explain how the FALCON Method can help you and what the newsletter contains, but for now, we'll focus on how you can use these principles yourself. Let's zoom in on the steps of the process I highlighted above to deepen your understanding along with your belief in this approach.

A Select Group of Top-Quality Companies

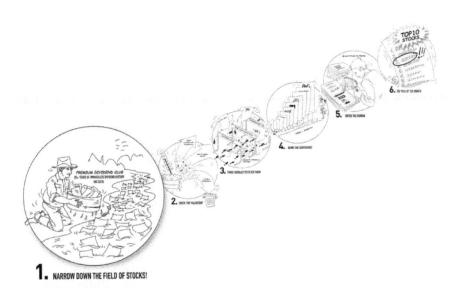

"The research of the past half-century showed that the tried and true clearly triumphed over the bold and new."

~ Jeremy Siegel[22]

After Prof. Siegel taught the world to love stocks in his book *Stocks for the Long Run*, he went on to study which companies provided the best investment returns. His mission was to identify the underlying factors of stellar performance so that he could create a recipe for successful stock selection. He made his latest findings available in another book, *The Future for Investors*, which is a fascinating read. Jeremy Siegel is one of a kind when it comes to his depth of data analysis. Even Warren Buffett speaks highly of his work, and for good reason!

"Jeremy Siegel's new facts and ideas should be studied by investors."

~ Warren Buffett

The conclusion of Siegel's study (backed up by tons of data) is that we should invest in the stocks of reputable, well-established companies that have been paying uninterrupted dividends for a long time. Trying to identify the next Google or simply falling victim to "sexy stock syndrome" is not the way to build wealth. Boring dividend-payers are the way to go if you are serious about your financial future. (Don't believe me? Read Siegel's book!)

"The importance of dividends in generating stock returns is not just historical happenstance. Dividends are the crucial link between corporate profits and stock values."

~ Jeremy Siegel[23]

Dividends don't lie; they cannot be cooked or falsified. A company either has money to pay the dividend or it doesn't. While earnings and even cash-flow numbers can be distorted by unfair practices, the dividend stands out as the single truly reliable item in corporate reports. If a company has been able to pay growing dividends for decades, it's a sure sign of its consistent earnings power. Taking this argument one step further, it is no surprise that companies with these characteristics tend to outperform. Let's see some proof!

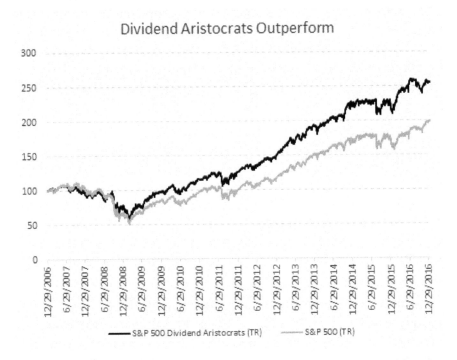

Dividend Aristocrats Outperform

The data in this chart comes from S&P Dow Jones Indices LLC[24]. The S&P 500 Dividend Aristocrats index shows an annualized total return of 9.66% over the 10 years examined, while the S&P 500 index—which serves the purpose of representing the whole stock market—came in at 6.97%. This is a very significant outperformance. Investing $10,000 at an annual return of 6.97% gets you $19,616 in 10 years, while investing the same amount with the 9.66% return takes you to $25,147. (Increasing the timeframe makes the gap even wider.)

If dividend aristocrats are that good, we clearly need to define what they are. Let's see what the S&P has to say about this: "The S&P 500Dividend Aristocrats measure the performance of S&P 500 companies that have increased dividends every year for the last 25 consecutive years. The index treats each constituent as a distinct investment opportunity without regard to its size by equally weighting each company."

As an investor, I have some problems with this index. First of all, why should I limit myself to only invest in stocks that are part of the S&P 500 index? This makes absolutely no sense to me—and fortunately, I am not alone with this opinion, so you can find ready-made databases[25] of stocks that have been paying growing dividends for a long time, but are not necessarily members of the S&P 500.

And this takes us to my second objection: Why is it so crucial that the company raises the dividend every single year? Corporate operations rarely follow a straight upward-sloping line, so I don't really mind if the management just keeps my dividend intact in difficult periods and goes back to raising it when the underlying operations offer some room for that. Wise managers would not sacrifice the overall health of the balance sheet just to keep an uninterrupted dividend-raising streak; however, they would do anything they could to continue paying the level of dividend they already promised, since their shareholders are expecting to receive that sum.

There may even be situations when investing some extra money in the future of the firm creates more shareholder value than increasing the dividend. Having seen corporate operations from the inside as a manager, I can personally come up with numerous reasons why increasing the dividend every single year might not always be sensible. As a result, I am perfectly satisfied with a long dividend history that shows no cuts, but a generally rising trend. Note that it isn't necessary to raise the dividend every year to fulfill my requirements!

Let me show you a hopefully eye-opening example of why I am not fascinated by annual dividend increases alone. You can see the dividend trends of Mercury General (MCY) and Boeing (BA) in the following chart. Notice that Mercury General is a Dividend Champion[26] with 30 straight years of higher dividends, while Boeing was nowhere near that respected status at the time of this writing, as it has the practice of keeping its dividends at the same level for some years before giving its investors a considerable raise. See the difference for yourself before I draw some conclusions!

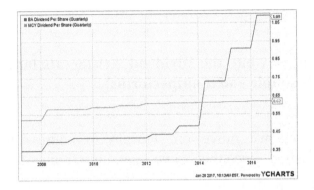

The management of Mercury General surely knows that even minuscule increases of the dividend can keep their company in the group of Champions, so they are doing just that[27]! However, recent increases came in below 1%, hardly a growth rate that makes investors salivate. Boeing, on the other hand, got kicked out of the dividend databases when it didn't raise its dividend for some time— but since then, its shareholders have enjoyed huge increases, the latest of which was 30%! I prefer to invest in companies in which the management employs capital wisely; when returns materialize in the form of increased cash generation, they know it is time to give me a considerable raise.

Why not buy the Dividend Aristocrats index? It's simple and it outperforms!

Before we move on, I want to address this question, since this is one I get quite frequently.

My problem with buying this index (or any index, for that matter) is that you are buying a basket of stocks. This means that you are buying the overpriced ones along with the reasonably priced and really cheap ones. I hate overpaying for something, so I prefer buying only those quality stocks that are available at good prices. I'd rather wait for the others until they're priced well, too.

The Dividend Aristocrats index is full of quality companies—there's no question about it! But quality alone is not enough to make a successful investment; you also need to pay attention to valuation.

1. ■ NARROW DOWN THE FIELD OF STOCKS!

The select group of stocks the FALCON Method focuses on includes the ones that have been paying a dividend for at least 20 years and did not cut it within this period. We never compromise about a company's immaculate dividend history.

> *"Many investors, especially those with a long-term perspective, prefer to receive a steadily growing rather than fluctuating level of dividends. A policy of continually raising the dividend commits management to meet specific return*

requirements of its shareholders. For this reason, we have also examined the 10 highest-yielding stocks among those that have not reduced their dividend in the last 15 years. A period of 15 years was chosen because that means the firm must have passed through at least one recession. Managements that have not cut their dividend have demonstrated the consistent earning power and strength of their corporations."

~ Jeremy Siegel[28]

Prof. Siegel found that the group of stocks described above tends to outperform. Basically, we need a long dividend history so that we can test how the company's management behaves when things get tough. Siegel uses a 15-year timeframe, while the FALCON Method goes for 20 years of immaculate dividend history. Notice also that the professor simply picked the highest yielding stocks from his select universe, while the FALCON Method uses a multi-faceted approach (the components of which are all proven). It is always good to see some serious data backing up an investment process, so thanks again to Prof. Siegel: we know that the FALCON Method is unquestionably on the right track!

Before summarizing this section and proceeding to the next step of the process, I want to remind you of an important thing most dividend investors completely miss: a company does not become a good investment target just because of its long and immaculate dividend record. **This dividend record is simply a telltale sign, a symptom that gives away how wonderful the underlying company is.**

Remember the black box model with all the money pipes? For a company to be able to pump more and more dividends through that output sub-pipe over the course of decades, it must have consistent earnings power—a really strong cash-generating business model. Having a long and immaculate dividend history is only a symptom of being a cash cow company where the management not only excels at maximizing operational efficiency but also caters to the shareholders' interests and treats them as partners. A company with such practices is the exact type of investment you should commit your capital to for the long run.

Now that you know that dividends are not the Eighth Wonder of the world but rather a decent telltale sign, you are head and shoulders above most investors out there.

To summarize: The FALCON Method focuses on a select group of stocks that have been paying dividends for at least 20 years and have not cut the dividend in this period. Companies qualifying for this list are reputable and widely known firms, so most investors feel comfortable buying and holding their stocks. Studies show that stocks with these qualities tend to outperform the market index and in addition to offering excellent total return potential, they also provide a reliable and growing passive income. Note that concentrating on this select group of companies alone is proven to tilt the odds in our favor—and we have hardly started the process of the FALCON Method yet!

It is important to understand that defining our "Premium Dividend Club" of stocks lays the foundation for consistent application of the strategy, as these shares are psychologically the easiest to hold onto (and even buy) in tough times. This pre-selection gives you serious extra power to stick with the strategy of the FALCON Method through thick and thin and enjoy its superb long-term performance. You may find the theory simple, but practice will prove that this last part is so important it is worth repeating over and over—this alone will determine your financial future. No matter the strategy you pick, you must stay the course and stick to the plan or you'll never win. Winners never quit and quitters never win. You have just received the greatest help possible to join the group of winners.

Double-Dip Benefit: Buy Them on the Cheap!

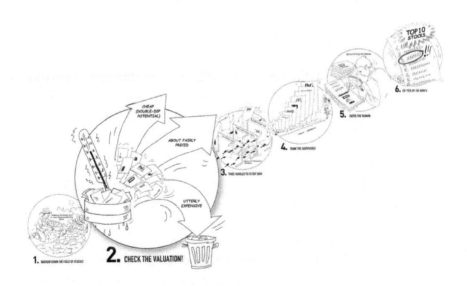

1. NARROW DOWN THE FIELD OF STOCKS!
2. CHECK THE VALUATION!
3. THREE HURDLES TO FILTER THEM
4. RANK THE SURVIVORS!
5. ENTER THE HUMAN
6. COP PICK OF THE MONTH

The FALCON Method aims for the highest possible total return while pocketing reliable and growing passive income in the form of dividends. To do this, it's best to know the building blocks of total return so that we can maximize our so-called "objective function."(Don't fret, I won't use math lingo along the way; I'll stick to simple explanations. After all, English is not even my mother tongue! Simply put: in order to maximize your total return, you must know its three parts.)

Let's see how your total return is made when you invest in stocks:

1. **Dividends**: Harvesting dividends throughout the investment timeframe means that money flows into your account regularly, so this must be a part of your total return. The higher the dividend you get compared to the capital you invest, the better. (We'll get back to the often-misunderstood point of dividend yield later.)

2. **Growth**: Imagine a company that is made up of 100 shares and makes a profit of $100 in Year1. In this case, the earnings per share (EPS) is $1[29]. In our example, the stock market attaches a value to this company that is usually 10 its profits, meaning that the whole company is worth $1,000 and one share is worth $10. This valuation multiple of 10 means that investors are willing to pay 10 years of earnings in advance (assuming there is no growth) to buy shares of this company.

   In a no-growth scenario with an unchanged valuation multiple, the company's value would be stuck at $1,000(the constant $100 earnings multiplied by the constant valuation multiple of 10).Now let's see what happens if our company switches to growth mode and manages to increase its earnings at an annual rate of 10%. In this case, by the end of the 10th year, the total profit grows to $259, while the earnings per share figure amounts to $2.59[30]. What is this company worth? What should its stock price be if the investors continue to value it at 10 earnings? Calculating with this fixed multiple gives us a share price of $25.90.

   A company that more than doubled its earnings (and could pay growing dividends) should have appreciated along the way. **Wherever earnings and dividends go, the stock price is sure to follow in the long run.** Having run through this simple example, I hope I have made it obvious that growing corporate income and cash generation can lift a company's stock price, thus contributing to your total return. After all, the capital you invested not only generated dividends but also appreciated nicely along the way.

3. **Valuation**: Why settle for the two return-generating engines outlined above when we can switch on the third one (the turbo-boost) as well? The stock market is made up of investors who are human beings with psychological biases, and this means that stock prices often deviate from the intrinsic value of the underlying companies they represent.

> *"Prices fluctuate more than values—so therein lies*
> *opportunity."*
> ~ Joel Greenblatt[31]

This means that we can sometimes buy the company in the above example for less than 10times earnings, so we can get its shares on the cheap side compared to the valuation level that was widely accepted historically. I feel this is the right point to bring up another simple illustration to regain your attention.

In the above example, considering a fixed valuation multiple of 10, you could make a profit of $25.90 - $10 = $15.90 on one share of the company. This means a return of 159% on your original investment[32]. Now imagine that a stock market panic hits in Year1 and frightened investors are flocking to unload their shares for $8 (instead of the "standard" $10).This means that you can make a purchase at a depressed valuation multiple of 8times earnings, as you only need to pay 8 years of the current profits instead of 10...if you dare!

"I will tell you how to become rich. Close the doors. Be fearful when others are greedy. Be greedy when others are fearful."

~ Warren Buffett

Let's see what happens if you were no chicken and, after determining that this company represents good quality and the price seems to be a bargain, you made the plunge and bought one single share (brave you!). The company grew its earnings per share to $2.59 within 10 years' time and the decade-old panic is long forgotten, which means that rational investors are once again happy to pay 10 earnings for your share. Seeing that you can sell this stock at $25.90, making a mighty profit of $17.90—which is a return of 224%—you begin to start thinking about position sizing; the amount of shares you should buy in a similar situation next time. (We'll cover that point in a bit.)

All I want now is for you to notice the huge difference in the return you could achieve (224% vs. 159%) by simply pulling the trigger when your target seemed to be available on the cheap side of historical valuation, meaning cheaper than usual!

Let's think about it more: just like stock prices can become depressed in times of panic, they can also become inflated in times of euphoria, when investors are more than ready to jump on the extraordinary opportunity that may be represented by your stock. In such cases, they are paying way more than the "standard" valuation multiple, thus boosting your return to such high levels that I'm not even willing to calculate them[33].

Now just breathe deep, take your time, relax, and think about the logic here. Imagine that the return-boosting effect of buying a quality company at a depressed valuation was not discovered by me, but by someone you can trust even with your eyes closed. In fact, by now you may be familiar with the name and message I quote below:

"Coca-Cola and Gillette are two of the best companies in the world and we expect their earnings to grow at hefty rates in the years ahead. Over time, also, the value of our holdings in these stocks should grow in rough proportion. Last year, however, the valuations of these two companies rose far faster than their earnings. In effect, we got a double-dip benefit, delivered partly by the excellent earnings growth and even more so by the market's reappraisal of these stocks. We believe this reappraisal was warranted. But it can't recur annually: we'll have to settle for a single dip in the future."

~ Warren Buffett in his Letter to Shareholders, 1991[34]

Here's an illustrative summary of all I detailed above:

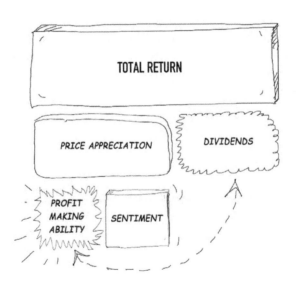

Your total return is made up of the dividends you receive (the more, the better) and the price appreciation of the stock. This price movement is mainly driven by the changing (and hopefully growing) profit-making capacity of the company: the more money it can generate, the more it is worth. However, there is one more component that influences the stock price and is totally unpredictable: market sentiment (represented by the valuation multiple). All you can do to put this extra wind in your sails is to buy quality assets when they seem to be priced cheaper than usual. Time will take care of the rest, since all storms eventually pass.

Before we move on, notice that there is a connection between the profit-making ability of the underlying company and the amount of dividends the stock can pay you. As a dividend is cash transferred to your account, it cannot be fabricated or falsified. In the long run, a company must generate enough cash to pay its shareholders or it has to cut its dividend.

This brings us to the point of dividend coverage or dividend safety that the FALCON Method examines in a later phase. (No dividend investing model can omit this factor! At least not without serious consequences.)

Now that you understand the forces operating in the background, all I need to say is that **this step of the process is about identifying which stocks on our list can be bought at below average valuation multiples, meaning that they may offer us a powerful double-dip benefit**.

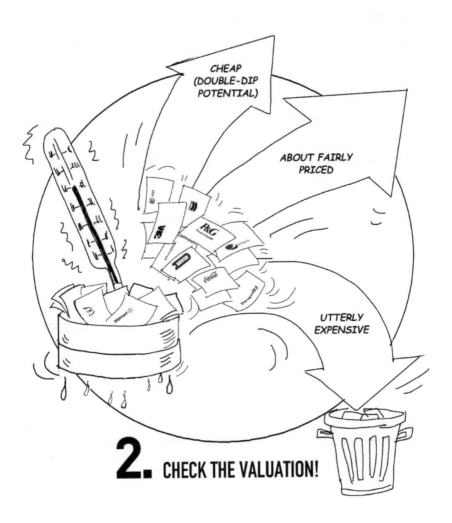

CHEAP
(DOUBLE-DIP
POTENTIAL)

ABOUT FAIRLY
PRICED

UTTERLY
EXPENSIVE

2. CHECK THE VALUATION!

You can imagine that at times of market euphoria, when investors are buying all the stocks they can get their hands on, there are many fewer stocks in our very strictly selected database that fit this criterion of double-dip potential, whereas during times of panic, there may be tons of them. I am sure, however, that regardless of the prevailing market conditions, it is always worth looking at this group of historically undervalued quality stocks because they undisputedly deserve a place on the list of targets for our following examinations. (In my experience, true gems can be uncovered this way.)

To show you that these principles of "historical undervaluation" and "buying on the cheap side of valuation" are not abstract ideas but a reality, let's look at the example of CVS Health (ticker symbol: CVS). For this purpose, I am utilizing FAST Graphs, which is one of the best tools I am aware of for illustrating the financial data of companies.

Take a look at the first scenario on the chart below, and then read on for some short explanations of what you see!

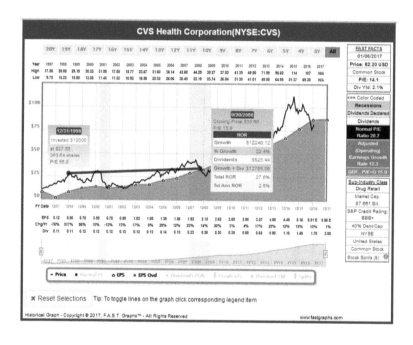

The large gray area shows the amount of profit CVS generates. Quite an impressive growth in the last 20 years, if you ask me! The line with the triangle markers indicates the price level that is calculated with a valuation multiple of 15[35]. For CVS, a multiple of 15 is considered to be the fair valuation in this model. Without elaborating (as that alone could fill another book), have a look at the black line, which is the stock price, and see how it tends to connect to the line with the triangle markers time and again after deviating from it. Long story short: if you buy CVS when the black line is above the line with the triangle markers, you are paying too much. And that's just what happened in this first scenario. (The purchase and sale are marked by the dots, which are connected by a thick line.)

As you see, the investor represented in this chart made a really questionable purchase of CVS stock at the end of 1998, paying 55 times earnings for the shares. (Notice that I said "an investor" and not you, since this is such a blunder that I don't want to offend you by presuming you'd make it!) Paying 55 times earnings, when 15 is considered the fair valuation multiple, is absolutely ridiculous.

For proof, let's see the result! By the end of September 2008, the earnings of CVS grew considerably (as the dark green area shows), but the price retreated to its fair value line, represented by the multiple of 15. So our hapless investor profited from the huge growth of the company and the collection of some decent dividends, yet still fell victim to the meaningful drop of the valuation multiple (from 55 to 15). As a result of these factors, his annual total return came in at a mere 2.5%. He invested in a wonderful company, but overpaid terribly! No excuses here; paying an extra high price can turn even the best company into a nightmare investment.

> *"No asset is so good that it can't become a bad investment if bought at too high a price."*
> ~ Howard Marks[36]

To get over this shocking misstep, let's turn to our second scenario, where we manage to buy the same CVS stock at a fair price. (Yes, this is "we," as buying such a quality company at fair value is something I happily admit to doing time and again.)

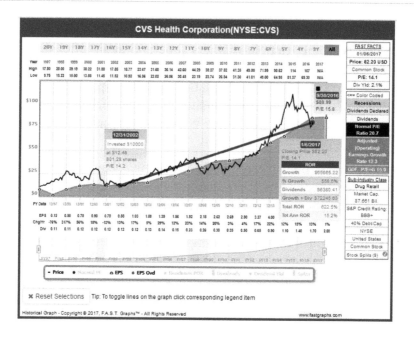

Simply put: we bought at a valuation multiple of 14.2 and sold at nearly the same multiple of 14.1, so we could profit from collecting the dividends and the growth of the underlying company, thus getting an annualized total return of 15.2%, which is pretty acceptable. The turbo-boost of multiple expansion was not turned on, but we still made a nice return on our money[37]. However, the step of the FALCON Method I am outlining here is all about turning on that extra boost, so let's see how we could do if we bought CVS stocks on the cheap!

This chart below encompasses a shorter timeframe, which is why it looks different at first glance. The selection of timeframes for the three scenarios is arbitrary, since I needed to pick entry and exit points that would illustrate the point.

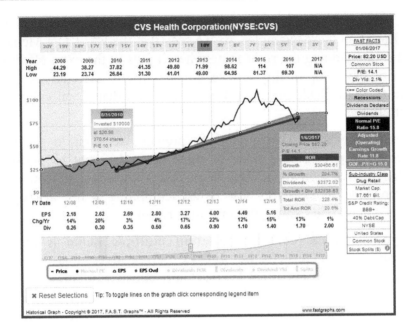

I will let the chart do the talking and just emphasize the main message. By pouncing on CVS shares when they were available at a bargain valuation of 10 earnings (10.1, to be more exact) and holding onto the shares until the beginning of 2017 when we unloaded them at a valuation multiple of 14.1, we made a great annualized return of 20.6%.

> *"As the saying goes, a stock well bought is half sold."*
> ~ Walter Schloss[38]

Long story short: if you can buy such a terrific company at cheaper than average prices, it is time to open your wallet. If I were you, I would read over the three annualized return figures in the above scenarios a few more times so it gets imprinted in my brain that buying extra-cheap is the recipe that brings extra profits, while paying an insanely high price can lead to disaster[39]. (In this first scenario, the enormous growth of the underlying company saved our anonymous investor, but not everyone gets away that lucky after overpaying, believe me!)

And here comes your favorite part: let's summarize things and move on! Based on these examples, we've seen that the FALCON Method is absolutely doing the right thing when it puts in the extra effort to identify those top-quality stocks on our strictly selected list that seem to be available on sale (meaning at lower than usual valuation multiples).

No matter what market conditions prevail, we want to see this special group of stocks and we most certainly want to perform further analysis on them. Based on this knowledge, it would be irresponsible to skip this test before compiling a list of Top10 stocks, yet no one I know of seems to perform it.

As you saw, the current valuation multiple alone is nearly meaningless—it has to be put in perspective. You need to compare it to the historical average fair valuation multiple, which can vary from stock to stock, and you are also advised to take the growth characteristics of the company into account when making a decision.

Depending on the market sentiment, there may be tons of top-quality companies on our list that seem to be undervalued, or there may be only a few of them. **The FALCON Method does not automatically exclude all stocks that are not deeply undervalued, but it most certainly prevents you from overpaying!** Buying at a fair valuation can be acceptable, though, as long as the underlying company is good.

> *"It's far better to buy a wonderful company at a fair price than a fair company at a wonderful price."*
> ~ Warren Buffett

In summary: By looking for the turbo-boost of depressed valuation, the FALCON Method can uncover true gems when the market presents them. It would be foolish to pass up such opportunities, so this step provides tremendous added value. (By the way, falcons are not said to be great at unearthing anything—even gems—but never mind! I've spent more time learning about investing than about wildlife...or anything else, for that matter.)

Threshold Criteria:
Should You Open Your Wallet at All?

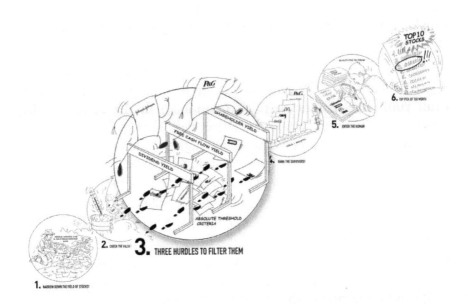

What if I told you to buy a stock that costs $100, where the underlying company has an annual (free) cash flow[40] of $1 per share (1% of the stock price) and pays a dividend of $0.50 per share (0.5% of the stock price)? To make things worse, the firm is continuously issuing new shares to further enrich its managers and finance their empire-building obsession, while still not producing any more money in spite of the growing company size.

You should say I'm crazy enough to be locked up in a dark room alone, and surely not allowed to share my views on investing at all!

I've just described a major difference between the absolute and relative aspects of valuation. This needs to be discussed a bit more before we move on to some very important criteria of stock selection.

For the sake of illustration, imagine that you are a very stubborn and simple-minded investor who is only interested in the stocks of Dividend Champions (companies with at least 25 straight years of higher dividends). So this is the well-defined group of your targets and you simply rank this group of stocks based on their dividend yield: the higher the better. Again, this would be foolish, but as simple as this example is, it will help us highlight something very important.

Think about this approach for a while and you should agree that **regardless of the prevailing market environment, you can always rank your chosen stocks (the Champions) in the order of the dividend yield they provide**. There will always be a highest-yielding Dividend Champion, a second highest, and a lowest as well. This is a relative ranking. You can produce this at any moment in time to see which stocks on your target list offer the best value (in this case, you only measure value by the dividend yield)—but notice that this does not mean the best-placed stocks in the ranking are always worth buying!

In times of market panic, stock prices get hammered and the dividend yield offered by Champions rises. This is when you can easily go for the "top of the ranking" companies.

But what happens when the other extreme strikes? At times of euphoria, stock prices get inflated and dividend yields can drop to irrationally suppressed levels. Imagine an extreme situation in which you do your ranking of Champions only to see that even the Top 10 only offer dividend yields below 1%. These are at the top of your "well-established" stock picking system, so should you go out and buy them? From the dark room where you've got me locked up, I am yelling as loud as I can: NO!

This is where some absolute criteria should come into play. We need to define certain thresholds where the failure to step over them absolutely disqualifies a stock, regardless of its place in the relative ranking. After all, if an investment opportunity can't offer decent prospects, you should keep your wallet shut and wait for better times to allocate your capital.

This step in the FALCON Method is all about defining those threshold criteria that should be met before any money goes out for investment. There are three things you should know before we proceed:

1. The indicators I picked are widely used ones, which have quantitative proof of being attached to superior stock performance. On the top of this, they are all reasonable, so it is easy to understand why they are important.

2. I deliberately define low limits with all the three indicators, since my experience shows that needing to meet all three low requirements at the same time usually disqualifies a very large chunk of stocks on our list, but leaves just enough of them to continue the analysis. So this is really a very tough combined filter despite seeming to be a bit lenient on the individual factors.

3. You cannot fix all the limits as absolute values for the rest of your life; this is why I will not disclose the current levels in this book. Please understand that the same dividend yield that looks attractive in a market environment when 10-year U.S. Treasuries yield below 2% can look ugly when risk-free rates approach 10%, so you should adjust your requirements accordingly. I am using this extreme example on purpose, just to make you think about and accept that your absolute criteria cannot be totally independent of the prevailing market

conditions. (Well, unless you are prepared to wait on the sidelines without investing for decades, speculating on certain macroeconomic developments, which is an approach no reputable value investor advocates.)

"We spend essentially no time thinking about macroeconomic factors. In other words, if someone handed us a prediction by the most revered intellectual on the planet, with figures for unemployment or interest rates or whatever it might be for the next two years, we would not pay any attention to it."

~ Warren Buffett

"I'm always fully invested. It's a great feeling to be caught with your pants up."

~ Peter Lynch[41]

Now let's see what the three threshold criteria actually are:

1. **Dividend yield**: This is calculated by dividing the forward 12-month dividend (what a stock is expected to pay in the year ahead) by the current market price[42]. This is totally intuitive: you want the highest possible dividend for the capital you invest.

   The serious mistake many dividend investors make is chasing yields: going for the highest yields available and losing sight of all other important criteria (like the safety of the dividend, for example).

   Let me repeat that the FALCON Method aims to provide the best possible total return (a completely different "objective function" than maximizing the current yield) while also targeting reliable and growing dividend income. Strategies that focus on maximizing the current yield often embarrass investors, since your significant other who looked attractive before the wedding can show his or her true colors after the ceremony (in the form of a huge dividend cut) and the marriage will either turn into a long agony or an extremely expensive divorce where the other party takes most of what you put into the relationship.

So on one hand, the FALCON Method does not accept ridiculously low dividend yields (compared to the prevailing market averages), but it also will not push this criterion to the limits. The falcon is wise enough to know that it will have further opportunities to weed out the surviving stocks in the latter phases of the process.

2. **Free cash flow yield**: This indicator is just as important as the dividend yield, although many dividend investors do not really consider it when allocating their capital. Free cash flow is a category that Warren Buffett made popular with the Appendix of his Letters to Shareholders in 1986. (I'm not going into details here, as Buffett himself does not suggest doing so: "I know that among our 6,000 shareholders there are those who are thrilled by my essays on accounting—and I hope that both of you enjoy the Appendix." Feel free to check out the 1986 letter online if you belong to this minority.)

Simply put: free cash flow measures the "no-strings-attached cash" that the company generates and does not need to spend on capital expenditures to keep its production capacity and competitive position[43].Basically, this is the money the company's management can freely decide how to allocate without sacrificing the company's overall future prospects. Free cash flow is the category that provides the basis for shareholder returns like dividend payments and stock repurchases. Although a company can finance these from its existing cash hoard or by taking on new debt, these sources only work temporarily. The true value of a business lies in its free cash flow generation and not the often distorted (or outright falsified) reported earnings figures.

"Our acquisition preferences run toward businesses that generate cash, not those that consume it. However attractive the earnings numbers, we remain leery of businesses that never seem able to convert such pretty numbers into no-strings-attached cash."

~ Warren Buffett, 1980[44]

The more dollars of free cash flow you get for your investment, the better, and this is exactly what the free cash flow yield measures[45].

Hoping that you still have some fading memories of the black box model with the money pipes, let me remind you that making excess cash is only one part of the equation. When purchasing shares in a company, you want to buy the most excess cash generation possible, and after that, pay close attention to the "what-will-they-do-with-the-money" factor (AKA capital allocation).

3. **Shareholder yield**: This filter addresses the dimension of capital allocation. Before committing my dollars, I want to see what percentage of my investment is returned to me, the shareholder. Dividends and share repurchases are both forms of shareholder return. While the first is self-evident, the second decreases the number of shares outstanding, thus increasing every remaining shareholder's ownership stake in the company (driving share prices higher).

   I like using the shareholder yield as a threshold criterion, as it helps filter out the firms that finance their dividends by issuing new shares[46]. (This is the previously mentioned "give Peter's money to Paul" practice.)

> *"At both BPL and Berkshire, we have never invested in companies that are hell-bent on issuing shares. That behavior is one of the surest indicators of a promotion-minded management, weak accounting, a stock that is overpriced, and—all too often—outright dishonesty."*
>
> ~ Warren Buffett, 2014[47]

For the sake of providing the most value possible here, I want to give you some additional info on this very powerful indicator. To tell you the truth, I was not a huge fan of the shareholder yield concept, since I always thought that its two components (dividends and share buybacks) are not simply additive. In fact, they are on totally different levels! On one hand, dividend announcements represent a strong promise for the future (especially if given by a company with an immaculate dividend history), while on the other hand, an announcement on prospective stock buybacks often stays just that—an announcement—and fails to materialize.

> *"Share repurchases often occur in a haphazard fashion. It is true that the price of a stock often responds favorably when management pledges that it will repurchase shares, but shareholders have a harder time monitoring whether management, in fact, is fulfilling its pledge. Various studies have concluded that a large percentage of announced share repurchases are not completed[48]. Often, management finds other uses for earnings, and not all of them are in the interest of shareholders."*
>
> ~ Jeremy Siegel, The Future for Investors, p. 152

Studies suggest there isn't much use in focusing on announced buybacks; in this category, the figures of the past (the TTM [trailing 12 months] buyback numbers) are what really matter because those are real. Based on this, I had the strange feeling that with one of my eyes, I was looking in the rearview mirror (the TTM buybacks of the past), while my other eye was fixated on the windscreen, looking ahead (at the future dividends). It made no sense to simply add these two numbers up. I was strong in my resistance until I read dozens of studies that highlighted the shareholder yield as one of the most powerful factors behind outperformance[49].

In their book Your Complete Guide to Factor-Based Investing, Andrew L. Berkin and Larry E. Swedroe elaborate on how investing in the stocks providing the best shareholder yield has outperformed both the market and the simple dividend-yield strategy in three out of the past four decades. The top-performing indicator is a three-component shareholder yield that includes net-debt paydown in addition to dividends and buybacks, where the net-debt paydown yield is measured as the year-over-year difference in the debt load of a firm, scaled by total market capitalization.

Let me remind you that the FALCON Method does not pursue a classic quantitative strategy, where you purchase the 20 stocks providing the highest shareholder yield, hold them for 12 months, and then repeat the process, selling all your stocks and buying the new darlings of the quant screener. This is very important to understand, as there must naturally be huge differences between a buy and hold strategy and a pure quant approach with high portfolio turnover. In the FALCON Method, we use the shareholder yield to uncover unfair practices, such as diluting current owners[50]. We favor companies with strong shareholder returns, meaning that besides paying a predictable and growing dividend, they are increasing our ownership stake by buying back stocks.

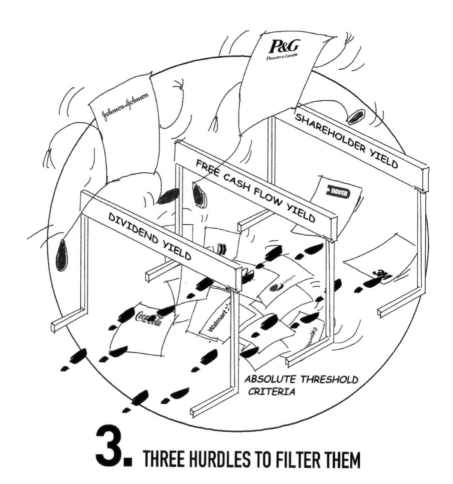

3. ■ THREE HURDLES TO FILTER THEM

Before moving on, I'll demonstrate the enormous value these three simple indicators can provide. Let's look at the data of three companies and draw some conclusions[51]!

Teva

Dividend Yield – 4.1%

Free Cash Flow Yield – 14.9%

Shareholder Yield – -5.4%[52]

Coca-Cola

Dividend Yield – 3.4%

Free Cash Flow Yield – 3.6%

Shareholder Yield – 4.7%

Target

Dividend Yield – 3.7%

Free Cash Flow Yield – 8.7%

Shareholder Yield – 15.2%

Although Teva has the highest dividend yield and its free cash flow yield looks great as well, the negative shareholder yield uncovers something I don't like: the company issued tons of shares, so it destroyed shareholder value instead of creating it. Whoever is mesmerized by the dividend yield fails to grasp the situation here! But the FALCON Method protects us from such blunders.

Coca-Cola is one of the favorite stocks of dividend investors—and rightly so. The dividend yield of 3.4% is considered attractive here (it is certainly above average for Coke), but if you have a look at how much free cash flow the company is generating for every dollar you invest, something not so nice dawns on you. Coke basically pays out nearly all of its cash flow in the form of dividends, which is not desirable. As the shareholder yield is slightly higher, you can assume that the company takes on some debt to buy back its stocks. These facts are all good to know before committing your capital.

Target offers a very competitive dividend yield of 3.7%, and the 8.7% free cash flow yield shows us that the retailer has much more room to increase its dividend than Coke because it pays out less than half of the cash it generates. On top of this, Target seems to be pretty active on the share repurchase front, as signaled by the 15.2% shareholder yield. Considering these numbers, Target seems to be the best choice from these three stocks.

This short demonstration highlights where defining the absolute minimum limits of three well-chosen criteria can take you. The FALCON Method easily separates the wheat from the chaff so that we only analyze the companies that are worth our time and effort. Stocks that are part of the carefully selected "Premium Dividend Club" and also meet these threshold criteria provide investment opportunities where you get decent value (and top quality) for your money. Now that we have them on a shortlist, it is time to rank them to see which are the best candidates for our portfolio!

Rank the Survivors

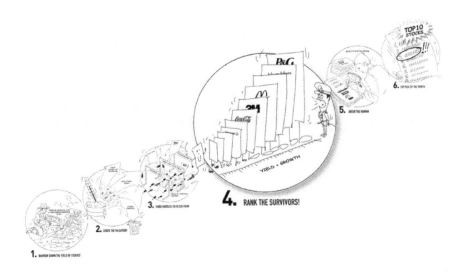

A t this point, we have a group of stocks with at least 20 years of immaculate dividend history—this alone tilts the odds in our favor. We have split the members of this "Premium Dividend Club" into two separate groups: those that are currently available at lower-than-usual valuation (offering a possible double-dip benefit) and those that are trading at fair or higher prices.

We will pay very close attention to the ones that are available on the cheap, as sometimes true gems can be uncovered among them. Nevertheless, we will not completely omit those members of the other group that are offered at about fair prices. (The rest of the "Premium Dividend Club" members are way too expensive, and since we know that quality and value are both required to make up a good investment opportunity, we won't compromise and will disqualify them for now.)

Below is an illustration how we treat stocks based on their current valuation levels.

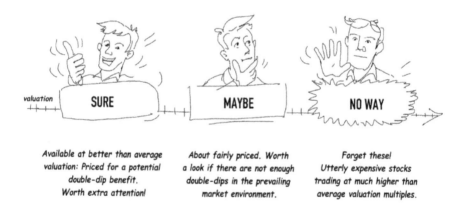

| Available at better than average valuation: Priced for a potential double-dip benefit. Worth extra attention! | About fairly priced. Worth a look if there are not enough double-dips in the prevailing market environment. | Forget these! Utterly expensive stocks trading at much higher than average valuation multiples. |

Knowing the difference between the absolute and relative aspects of valuation, we drew up some absolute threshold criteria that any investment opportunity should meet to earn our capital. We show no mercy and also disqualify all the stocks in the "Sure" and "Maybe" groups that fail to meet our threshold criteria.

Now that we are done with all these steps, pretty much any company that is still standing can be considered a good investment. But we want to see which the best candidates are, so it is high time to carry out a relative ranking! (Notice that the FALCON Method does this only when the field of stocks has been narrowed down to the very best. Relative ranking has its place in a good investment process, but it shouldn't come first.)

Because the FALCON Method aims to maximize your total return, it is no surprise that the factors it uses for the ranking all come from the total return equation that you're now familiar with. (As a quick refresher: the total return is influenced by the dividend yield, the growth, and the change of the valuation multiple.) As the last component, the multiple, has already been addressed in our process, let's turn our focus to the dividend yield and growth!

These two go hand-in-hand and should never be analyzed separately (a sin many investors commit). A stock that provides a low dividend yield as a starter should be able to grow and increase its dividend at a high rate; otherwise, it cannot become an attractive investment. Would you put your money into a stock that offers a dividend yield of 2% and an annual growth of a mere 2%? Hopefully not[53]! For a low yielder like that to get your attention, it must show enormous growth potential, like 10% or more annually[54].

On the other hand, a high yielder has already built something of a case for itself by offering a starting yield of, say, 5%. This is the dividend you are almost sure to receive, so a less spectacular growth rate could be enough on top of this to provide a decent total return. (If you are not entirely comfortable with these last two paragraphs yet, I suggest that you play with the calculator at Miller/Howard Investments[55] for a few minutes—the connection between the current yield and growth rate will become obvious. You can compare an imaginary low yielder and a high yielder, for example, to illustrate what I have been explaining.)

In the example on the next page, I used CVS Health (CVS) and AT&T (T), two stocks offering totally different yield and growth profiles at the moment. Again, feel free to use the calculator at the link below the chart to create your own examples!

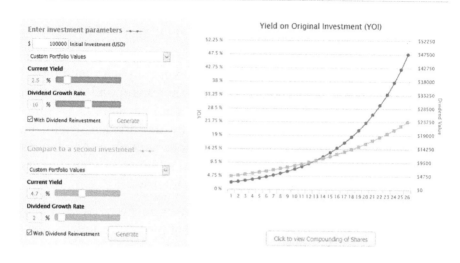

Source: https://sugar.mhinvest.com/highcharts/investment.php

Examining the current yield and the dividend growth rate together is not an innovation at all! And it's always good when we don't have to reinvent the wheel, something falcons aren't known for excelling at.

Dividend investors often use the so-called "Chowder Rule" to determine which stocks offer the best starting yield and growth combination. The Chowder Rule is really simple; it just adds up the stock's current dividend yield and its trailing 5-year dividend growth rate to determine if the mix of value and growth warrants a timely buy. The higher the number, the better. In practice, this is how most dividend investors use the Chowder Rule:

1. For stocks offering a dividend yield of 3% or higher, the sum of the dividend yield and the trailing 5-year dividend growth must be at least 12.
2. If the current dividend yield is less than 3%, the sum of the dividend yield and the trailing 5-year dividend growth must be at least 15 (to offset the risk that comes from the higher growth expectations with low yielders).
3. There is a separate set of rules for utility stocks.

While I like the core concept behind the Chowder Rule, I also have some problems with applying it without thinking. First and foremost: Why should we focus on the trailing 5-year dividend growth rate alone? If the growth rate shows some signs of a recent slowdown, the 5-year rate can mask this and distort our opinion about the stock. If we can have a look at the dividend growth rates of different time horizons, then why not go for this more realistic picture?

> For example, the retailer Target (TGT) had a 5-year average dividend growth rate of 16% as of early 2017, as it used to raise its dividend by 20% for some years. However, the FALCON Method highlights that the last two raises came in at 7–8%. No company can keep up a growth rate of 20% forever, and even the management of Target honestly says that they have reached the payout ratio they are comfortable with (by intentionally raising the dividend faster than the underlying business grew for a certain period). So from this point on, the dividend growth rate will correspond with the earnings growth, which is expected to be somewhere in the mid-single-digit range. It would be a huge mistake to blindly pick the Chowder number, as it fails to grasp the whole picture I have just outlined. The FALCON Method would never make such a mistake, and hopefully using it will save you from such costly blunders too. (Of course, you cannot know the story behind every single stock, but numbers do tell the story if you pick the factors of your model wisely!)

Secondly, I understand that low yielders carry additional risk, since in the dreaded scenario when high growth expectations fail to materialize, these stocks can turn out to be subpar investments. It is absolutely justified to demand a higher Chowder number in the group of low yielders, but I would not arbitrarily split the universe of stocks in two based on a fixed yield level of 3% that fails to take the prevailing interest rate environment into account.

So I like the underlying mechanics of the Chowder Rule but would never use it the way its massive follower base typically does. Instead, **the FALCON Method looks at different timeframes for**

gauging a company's dividend growth rates and compiles Chowder-like numbers based on these growth rates. All these "yield plus growth" types of indicators (encompassing different timeframes) serve as separate factors that each receive a weighting, allowing us to carry out a multifactor weighted ranking process. This means that the FALCON Method takes into account all the available dividend growth data, beyond the current yield, and combines them in one powerful indicator we can use to rank the stocks that are still standing.

HOW DOES A WEIGHTED MULTIFACTOR RANKING WORK? A QUICK EXAMPLE

For the sake of simplicity, imagine we only have stocks A and B in our universe. Our model uses three factors for ranking these stocks. The first step is to calculate the value of the factors we use. (A factor can be the dividend yield, the Chowder number, the price-to-earnings ratio, or anything that makes sense to you.) Let's say the results are as follows[56]:

Factor 1	Factor 2	Factor 3
Stock A – 23.3%	Stock A – 34.5%	Stock A – 24.6%
Stock B – 27.3%	Stock B – 27.0%	Stock B – 25.6%

Now that we have these values, the next question is, what weight should we assign to these factors? In this case, we opt for equal weighting, which means that all factors will receive a weighting of 33.3%—thus, the three of them make up 100%. (You could pick any three numbers, the sum of which equals 100 percent.)

The last step is to do the calculation for the ranking. For "Stock A," it is the following: 33.3% x 23.3% + 33.3% x 34.5% + 33.3% x 24.6% = 27.47

For "Stock B": 33.3% x 27.3% + 33.3% x 27% + 33.3% x 25.6% = 26.63

If you rank these two stocks based on the scores you have just calculated, "Stock A" comes out slightly ahead.

The weighted multifactor quantitative ranking process works this way, but can have many more than three underlying factors; it can assign different weights to all of them and, of course, it needs to calculate the scores for all the stocks in the universe it examines and then rank them accordingly. (If not all of your factors can be expressed as percentages, some additional work is required. Fortunately, the FALCON Method does all this for you.)

4. RANK THE SURVIVORS!

By applying this unbiased quantitative technique and selecting Chowder-like numbers with different timeframes as the ranking factors, our approach tackles the mistake of arbitrarily picking the 5-year number and drawing an incorrect conclusion from that simple figure (like many people do).

On the top of this, I see no reason to determine absolute threshold levels based on Chowder-like numbers. Instead, the FALCON Method uses them for the purpose of relative ranking only. It is hard to make a mistake this way, since all I say is "the higher the Chowder numbers, the better," and this statement isn't easy to dispute if one understands the underlying logic I have outlined so far.

Notice that our investment approach acknowledges that a lower yielder must provide higher growth to become an excellent investment, while a high yielder can offer great returns with lower growth rates. As the FALCON Method examines the Chowder-like numbers of different timeframes, **it penalizes companies where the growth rate fell recently or which failed to raise their dividend for some years.** (Remember Mercury General, the company that operated with minuscule raises to preserve its Champion status? Such gimmicks won't get it anywhere in the FALCON Method: without serious dividend growth, it falls to the bottom of our list, even if it managed to survive until this round[57].)

Remember, this weighted multifactor ranking process is applied to all the stocks in the "Premium Dividend Club:" both those that offer a potential double-dip benefit by being available on the cheap and those that are fairly or more expensively priced. Candidates that don't meet our absolute threshold criteria (dividend yield, free cash flow yield, and shareholder yield) are disqualified regardless of which group they belong to. We make no compromise here, since their prices are simply too high to offer decent returns for a sensible investor.

By now we have narrowed down the list of stocks considerably, and for good reason! **The last step of the FALCON Method involves some qualitative judgment, which means it is labor intensive. Only the most promising stocks on our list deserve this kind of treatment.** This is why we start with the seemingly undervalued survivors that rank high based on "yield plus growth" characteristics. (Notice that these are companies with immaculate dividend histories of at least 20 years. In these cases, the multiple expansion—or reversion to the mean, to be more exact—can work in our favor, boosting our return, while the current yield and growth figures together indicate an excellent total return potential. All three components of the total return equation are our allies, so it is hard to imagine a better position than this.)

After stocks with double-dip potential, we also examine the fairly priced candidates in the last phase of our selection process in order to compile the best Top10 list possible under the prevailing market conditions. Now let's see what this final phase involves and how the

FALCON Method puts the finishing touches on this well-rounded stock selection process!

10

Final Round:
Enter the Human

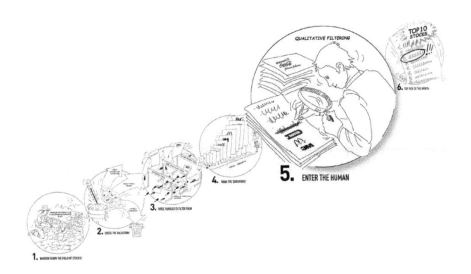

Until now, the FALCON Method followed quantitative discipline. All its decisions were numbers-based, totally eliminating psychological biases from the investment process. Although some subjectivity crept in when deciding which stocks were "about fairly valued" based on the historical multiples[58], decisions made at that stage do not have a huge influence on the final outcome of the model.

But now that we have a ranking of the stocks that seem to be the very best investment candidates, it's time to have a look at them from a more qualitative point of view. This is where human judgment and emotions come into play, so please notice that the FALCON Method only lets these forces29 out when it is almost impossible to screw things up, as only stocks with great attributes remain standing.

This phase of the process means that the FALCON Method is about 90% quantitative and 10% qualitative. Closely examining the candidates that ranked well gives me peace of mind that I have done my job and applied all the knowledge I've accumulated throughout the years. Although this human element may not provide empirically proven added benefits, it is worth including for this "peace of mind" effect alone, which can seriously influence how an investor behaves in the times of panic. Now, instead of overexplaining this, let's have a look at some points I am focusing on in this phase.

DIVIDEND COVERAGE

It is always worth examining the safety of the dividend. Payout ratios can tell the story, so I look at the classic dividend-per-share/earnings-per-share ratio as well as the more meaningful dividend-per-share/free-cash-flow-per-share ratio. The latter is more important, as dividends can only be paid from cash and not some fabricated earnings. You may notice that the FALCON Method has already examined dividend safety indirectly along the way. We had absolute threshold criteria for both the dividend yield and free cash flow yield, so in an indirect way, we addressed the relationship of dividends and free cash flow as well.

I believe the dividend coverage ratios are not suitable for quantitative ranking purposes because it's not guaranteed that a company that pays out 40% of its free cash flow is better than one with a 60% ratio. I don't determine any strict ceilings for disqualification, either, because companies can have very different business models that explain their payout ratios—this is where human judgment comes into play instead of rigid filtering criteria.

> Philip Morris is a fantastic company if you put the ethical concerns relating to the business aside. Even Warren Buffett agrees with me on this: "I'll tell you why I like the cigarette business. It costs a penny to make. Sell it for a dollar. It's addictive. And there's fantastic brand loyalty."

> The company's management decided that they would pay out almost all the free cash flow it generates in the form of dividends, so their payout ratio is intentionally high. Knowing their business model and their fantastic dividend history, I wouldn't disqualify this stock based on some payout ratio criterion alone. Doing so simply makes no sense.

Do you remember the example of Coca-Cola? This Dividend Champion met all our absolute threshold criteria and yet still failed to make the grade. The main reason for sweeping it aside was the deterioration of its dividend coverage, which resulted from increasing the dividend at a higher rate than the growth of the underlying business would allow[59]. At the moment, Coke yields 3.4%, but this is all it can provide because its payout ratios are overextended[60]. The FALCON Method can identify much better investment opportunities.

So on the one hand, I try to avoid very high payout ratios, while on the other hand, I tend to look at the company's business model in dubious situations. This step cannot be automated wisely; this is why it is carried out in this last human-based phase.

RETURN ON INVESTED CAPITAL (ROIC)

> *"It will continue to be the objective of management to improve return on total capitalization (long-term debt plus equity)…"*
> ~ Warren Buffett, 1971

When you invest money, you want the best returns possible. If you become a shareholder in a company, the equity corresponding to your ownership stake in the company is your money. It is worth paying attention to how well the management employs the capital at its disposal. If the return figures are low, you may have the feeling that you could do something better with your money than leaving it in the company where it will compound at unsatisfactory rates.

I focus on the ROIC indicator[61], which incorporates the long-term debt part of the company's capital in addition to the equity, since that is capital the management puts to work; thus, it should earn decent returns on it. It goes without saying that the higher the ROIC, the better.

This part of the process also addresses the indebtedness of the firm. I don't believe in absolute leverage criteria like debt-to-equity. Again, companies can have very different business models and these affect such ratios. High leverage alone is not a problem until the return on invested capital considerably exceeds the interest rate on debt. For instance, if management uses the money it raised from debt to earn an annual return of 15% while paying an interest rate of 2–3%, it can create huge value for its shareholders. I surely wouldn't penalize them for such sensible maneuvers (as long as they do not take it to extremes).

While the combination of high leverage and low returns can be lethal, this question is never black or white, so coming up with an answer requires human judgment. Even quantitative studies reveal that companies that use very little or no debt can offer subpar returns just like their overleveraged counterparts[62]. The key is striking some healthy balance.

Notice that if you have the chance to examine the three-component shareholder yield, which is the one that incorporates net debt paydown along with dividends and share buybacks, you are examining the debt question from two different angles. Although the FALCON Method sets no specific criteria for leverage, it pays close attention to the most important aspects of the company's indebtedness.

IS IT CYCLICAL?

"Making a huge bet on a cyclical business, which turns on the price of a commodity, to me is a reckless way to invest money."

~ Glenn Greenberg[63]

Before I influence you in any way here, please have a quick look at the 20-year earnings charts of two companies: V.F. Corporation and Chevron.

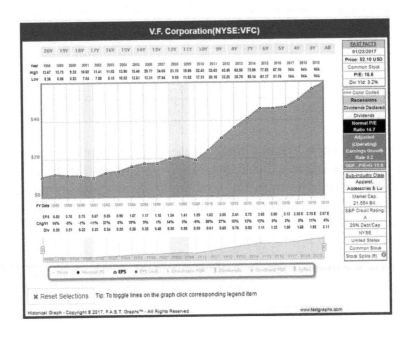

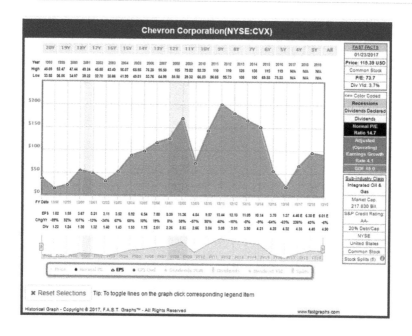

Even if you know nothing about these firms, it should be obvious that they have entirely different business characteristics. While V.F. Corporation benefits from the continuous demand for its powerful brands, including Timberland, Eastpak, Vans, The North Face, Lee, Wrangler, etc., Chevron is involved in the much more volatile—yet highly lucrative—oil business.

Chevron's earnings and cash flow fluctuate wildly, whereas V.F. Corporation has a much more predictable operation. I will not tell you that a cyclical business is always a bad choice, but it requires some additional considerations before investing.

Oddly enough, cyclicals are cheap at the bottom of the cycle, when their valuation multiples seem to be extra high (because of the earnings collapse), and they can get pretty expensive at the peak of the cycle, when multiples look much better as a result of skyrocketing earnings. I have read quite a bit on this topic and what I learned can be distilled as follows: Investing in cyclicals is often counterintuitive, so it requires careful consideration.

Suffice it to say that no quantitative model is able to handle this task, this is why it is essential to take a close look at the companies near the top of our ranking and determine which of them are cyclicals that are thus in need of some extra attention.

WHAT IS MY CONSERVATIVE ESTIMATE OF TOTAL RETURN?

"It is better to be approximately right than precisely wrong."

~ Warren Buffett

Based on dividends, future earnings, and changes in the valuation multiple, it's possible to come up with a rough figure of expected annual total return for any stock. There are two important things to know about this: first, no matter how hard you try, this can never be anything more than an estimate; accuracy is not only impossible, but shouldn't even be aimed for. Second, being very conservative is the key to successfully apply this step. Investing is all about margin of safety, as Ben Graham taught!

"Confronted with a challenge to distill the secret of sound investment into three words, we venture the motto, Margin of Safety."

~ Benjamin Graham[64]

Tweaking the numbers can be both fun and useful if you know what you are doing, have solid background knowledge in investing, and love what you are doing. However, things can go wrong if you attach too much importance to the prevailing stories of the stocks you analyze and persuade yourself not to buy the top-quality stuff that is currently hated by the majority of investors. (That's why it is on sale, after all. The exact time to buy is when others are fearful, but doing so is easier said than done.)

A second potential mistake stems from taking yourself too seriously and becoming overconfident in your analytical (or, rather, future-predicting) abilities. On one hand, I would never leave out the step of conservative total return evaluation, but on the other hand, I would not over-appreciate the inputs it can give me. By this, I mean that estimates of total returns are not exact enough for ranking purposes, although they can help eliminate the candidates that clearly fall short of our rational expectations. Whichever data provider or visualization tool you choose, this will be a step where you need to put your mind to work.

5. ENTER THE HUMAN

By the time I go through the steps of the FALCON Method, I feel totally comfortable investing in the stocks that rank best and already have passed all the quantitative and qualitative criteria. This process looks at companies from many different angles, encompassing "the black box model with the money pipes" and leaving no room for the mistake of omission.

As a result, we can compile a list of Top10 stocks that provide the best investment opportunities at the current moment. Beyond this, as part of the FALCON Method, I also highlight a "Top Pick," which is the company that I myself would pick if I could only invest in one stock.

How Can the FALCON Method Help You?

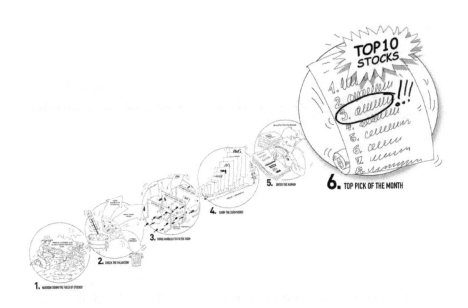

By now, I hope I have been able to show you some aspects of stock selection you may not have thought about before. And hopefully I was able to present everything in such an easy-to-understand format that you might be wondering why you haven't followed this method so far just based on its common-sense nature.

At this point, you may feel you have learned something completely useful here and are ready to start implementing all this stuff on your own. When you do, you will encounter many obstacles (e.g., expensive or outright bad data providers of stock info), but you can reach your goal if you are devoted and never give up. I have gone through this process myself, so I should sound credible when I warn you in advance: this will cost you thousands of dollars and many months of your time. If investing is your passion, you may opt for this first option, although I feel your money and energy could be much better spent.

The second option is to get the targeted results of this investment process in a ready-to-use newsletter format every month. The *FALCON Method Newsletter* includes the following valuable sections:

- **An introduction:** Here I share my opinion on the market, highlight some current news and opportunities worth paying attention to, or simply illustrate an important investment concept with current examples. By reading this, subscribers to the *FALCON Method Newsletter* will become better investors and decision makers.

- **The Top10:** This is exactly what you think it is—the list of the 10 highest ranked stocks that survived all the method's filtering processes and met all our quantitative and qualitative criteria.

- **Short analyses:** For all the companies in the Top10, I share the most important data and considerations in the form of an easy-to-understand analysis. This part is meant to help you understand my thought process, along with the background of the investment opportunities the FALCON Method has highlighted.

- **Top pick of the month**: When compiling the newsletter and distilling all the details of the month's top stocks, the best opportunity usually stands out from the rest of the pack. I feel it provides added value if I tell you which company I would invest in if I could only go with one stock. (If it is a close call between two candidates, I will let you know my thoughts about why I picked the winner. This is both educational and useful.)

- **A complete ranking of all the stocks in the "Premium Dividend Club"**: In this section, you get a list of stocks with at least 20 years of immaculate dividend history, ranked in the order of their yield-plus-growth characteristics as described in the "Rank the Survivors" part above. This list highlights the stocks that fail to meet the absolute threshold criteria of the FALCON Method so you can omit them if you wish. You can use this ranking if you are as obsessed with undervaluation and the double-dip benefit as I am, since this ranking does not employ the double-dip filter in order to include all the stocks of the "Premium Dividend Club". You can also see the broad business sector in which the listed companies operate, which can help balance your portfolio. Some subscribers may find this useful, so why not provide it?

- **When to sell**: The FALCON Method is not a trading system, but a buy and hold approach, so it employs very simple rules for selling that are not often triggered. In the newsletter, I always give an alert when one of the stocks that in some previous issue occupied a place in the Top10 becomes a "sell."

There are two reasons for selling a stock under the FALCON Method: the company cut its dividend or its shares have become extremely overvalued. If neither of these happen, it is better to leave the stock alone. Our attitude corresponds with the teachings of Ben Graham, as we know we should forget about our stocks as long as they are doing their job: growing their earnings and putting more and more dividends in our pockets. We are very picky when it comes to stock selection in the first place, but we only focus on the dividend and valuation criteria afterwards.

"Keep your eyes wide open before marriage, half shut
afterwards."
~ Benjamin Franklin[65]

With the *FALCON Method Newsletter*, you are not buying excitement but performance. The difference between these two is night and day.

Let me share some eye-opening research results with you. Financial services giant Fidelity reportedly conducted an internal study, a performance review of clients' accounts, to see which accounts did the best. They found that the best-performing investment accounts were from investors who were either dead or had completely forgotten that they had accounts at Fidelity.

Hard ways to become successful indeed, but don't worry—simply staying passive can do the trick! The problem is, most people believe that activity is rewarded, so they think they always have to *do* something to get top results. Well, it is good to know that this is not so in the field of investing.

"Our portfolio shows little change: We continue to make more
money when snoring than when active. Inactivity strikes us as
intelligent behavior."
~ Warren Buffett, 1996[66]

Practicing passivity is easier said than done, although it clearly protects us from taxes, transaction costs, and our psychological biases, all of which are enormous drags on long-term investment performance. The simple yet effective selling rules of the FALCON Method keep us on the proven track of passivity and outperformance.

I want to make something very clear before I even mention the price of the *FALCON Method Newsletter*: I am not selling some entertaining "show business" stuff here, so don't expect me to come up with 10 brand-new stock ideas each and every month! I am putting my money where my mouth is, so I myself invest in the stocks that are ranked best by the FALCON Method. I am experienced enough to accept that I should always limit my purchases to the best opportunities Mr. Market provides, no matter how slowly or quickly he changes the names of the stocks on sale. Although I have absolutely no control over the market, I have total control over my own decisions. Following the path I have outlined here, one can build a diversified portfolio of the best stocks in various sectors. This takes time and the process is more rewarding than exciting.

> *"Investing should be like watching paint dry or watching grass grow. If you want excitement, go to Las Vegas."*
> ~ Paul Samuelson[67]

I have always felt I can use the money I make to buy excitement if I wish, so why seek excitement in the field of investing, where it is simply too expensive or overpriced to get? (And a sensible investor does not buy overpriced stuff.)

12

The Price:
How Much Can You Save?

"Price is what you pay, value is what you get."
~ Warren Buffett

I have spent years reading all the books and newsletters on investment I could get, as learning everything about this field is my passion. After a while, the pieces of the jigsaw puzzle started to come together and I found I could synthesize all the information I learned and thought important. This is how the FALCON Method was born.

The most eye-opening experience came when I had the chance to speak at a financial conference in 2016; the audience of about 300 people surrounded me after the presentation. They acknowledged that they understood and enjoyed my presentation, and the investment process I drew up seemed logical, but many of them had the exact same question for me: "I see that you love what you're doing and you must be good at it. **How can I benefit from this concept without putting in the same amount of work you did? Couldn't you just share the names of the stocks you consider the best investments?**"

That was when I decided that I should write this book describing the underlying process of the FALCON Method and start a newsletter service that offers people just what they are asking for: the stocks that stand out from the crowd and provide the best investment opportunities. My main motivation was to make this service available to as many people as possible.

I can tell you honestly that such a comprehensive process as the FALCON Method requires huge amounts of data, all structured and illustrated in a certain way so that one can manage the group of hundreds of stocks that make up the "Premium Dividend Club". **These tools together cost me $1,318 annually as of January 2017.** (And the prices of the underlying services are trending up.)

Even if you are willing to put in all the work yourself, you may not have a portfolio size that makes paying more than $1,000 annually for data and visualization services reasonable. And this is just the money part of the equation—the value of your time and effort is hard to quantify.

I had a serious decision to make about pricing. I did not want to create an "elite service" for just a few people who could afford the high standard I am committed to providing. So instead of looking at my costs and time invested, I examined the pricing of other investment newsletters, regardless of their (often subpar) quality. I noticed that **typical annual subscription rates ranged from $79 to $795.** At this point, I did a quick survey among the attendees of my above-mentioned presentation and was amazed to find that most of them said they would be happy to pay somewhere in the region of $250–300 per year to receive the monthly picks of the FALCON Method and my related analyses.

Considering this was after they met me in person and had gained an impression I couldn't make with this book (or could I?), I thought I would make your decision really easy. **I set the annual subscription rate of the *FALCON Method Newsletter* at $197**.

And although it's already deeply below the real value of the service, this is still not my final offer, since I want to show you how much I appreciate that you have read this far. Understanding the background of the FALCON Method is essential to sticking with it for the long run, and it is the only way my newsletter can benefit you. In an ideal world, I would only have subscribers who took the time to study my investment process, so I would like to thank you for doing just that. **As a welcome bonus, your annual subscription rate is reduced to $97 (or about $8 a month) if you use the coupon code "READITALL30." You will be shielded from future price hikes as well; your rate will stay the same as long as you continue your subscription without interruption.**

As I believe in the old-school way of doing business, I answer all the subscriber questions I receive. So honestly, a bit of selfishness crept in when I offered you this low price, since I think it's better to surround myself with a group of people who are familiar with what the FALCON Method is about than with ignorant ones who devote no time to learning and understanding the basics but want instant wealth instead.

There are situations in the stock market when the price you pay and the value you get diverge considerably, as Warren Buffett frequently mentions. Good investors pounce on the opportunities that let them buy great value at a deep discount. Having read this far, you now realize that the *FALCON Method Newsletter* can be the cornerstone of your financial future and is worth much more than $8 a month. Feel free to use the coupon code below and enjoy the results of your first value purchase. Welcome on board!

> Visit the page *thefalconmethod.com/newsletter-30day-special* to join now and instantly receive the latest FALCON Method Newsletter.
> (Enter coupon code READITALL30 on the checkout form)
> Price: ~~$197~~ $97 annually

As a special offer for reading this book your plan comes with a risk-free 30-day trial (instead of the standard 7-day version). You are truly not billed for 30 days, so there is no downside at all to trying the *FALCON Method Newsletter*, while there is a serious upside to investing in high-quality dividend-paying stocks.

How to Use the Newsletter Wisely

uilding a high-quality stock portfolio is absolutely not complex. However, depending on your situation, there may be alternative ways to put the recommendations of the FALCON Method to good use.

If you are saving and investing regularly, it is a wise strategy to see which stocks in the Top 10 you have the least dollar amount invested in, then buy the highest ranked of those stocks. Or you can go for the Top Pick of the month if you do not own it yet. With this approach, you can build a well-diversified portfolio of top-quality stocks, all purchased at attractive prices. (Of course, you also can use the Top10 list as a simple idea generator if you want to analyze companies on your own.)

If you have a lump sum to invest, I suggest that you divide the money into 24 equal parts and invest it gradually over the next 24 months (putting in 1/24 of the money each month), always purchasing the most attractive stocks on the Top10 list of the

FALCON Method Newsletter. This way, you can free yourself from the frustration of the Mission: Impossible called market timing.

> *"I can't recall ever once having seen the name of a market timer on Forbes' annual list of the richest people in the world. If it were truly possible to predict corrections, you'd think somebody would have made billions by doing it."*
>
> ~ Peter Lynch[68]

You may also have your own criteria, like "the dividend yield must be above 3%." In this case, pick the stocks from the Top10 that fulfill your requirements, and do this every month. But if you notice that none of today's best opportunities can jump over your bar, it may be time to think whether your expectations are still realistic in the prevailing market environment. (You can always go for high yielders, but if the market is not in the mood to support your passion, you will have to make a serious compromise on quality that can easily backfire. The FALCON Method will show you the best ideas in every kind of market.)

No matter whether you intend to invest regularly or have a lump sum now, you must make a decision about how many stocks you want to own in your portfolio. You can read numerous arguments for both diversification and portfolio concentration. Let me clear up this issue once and for all by highlighting the two opposite ends of the spectrum. These extreme examples will help you draw the right conclusion.

- If you are a theoretical "know-everything" investor who is 100% sure which one single stock in the whole universe will provide the highest return, it would be a dumb move to put any money into even your second-best idea. In this theoretical case, you should go for total concentration and put 100% of your money into that single best stock.

- On the other hand, if you are a "know-nothing" investor who wants to profit from the wealth-building power only stocks can provide, you should put your eggs in as many baskets as possible. After all, you know nothing about specific companies, so how could you pick any of them and expect superior performance?

Professional investors who analyze companies deeply, read all their filings, and immerse themselves in industry data are often running concentrated portfolios, since they spend all their lives studying stocks and closely following the performances of the underlying businesses. Warren Buffett is certainly this type of investor, but you will most likely not follow in his footsteps.

A few years ago, Warren Buffett was speaking to students of the Columbia University School of Business when he was asked what the biggest key to success was that he could share with the class. His answer was surprising, to say the least.

He held up a stack of reports and trade publications he had brought with him and said, "Read 500 pages like this every day. That's how knowledge works. It builds up like compound interest. All of you can do it, but I guarantee not many of you will do it."

Chances are you won't become the next Warren Buffett, and you most likely should not aim for a highly concentrated portfolio, but you can still beat the market if you strike a balance between the two extremes. **My suggestion is to go for 20–30 positions and make them approximately equally weighted.** This way, you will reap the rewards of diversification[69] where you can have a portfolio of top companies from various sectors, and these stocks will put ever-increasing dividends in your pocket.

If you start following the recommendations of the *FALCON Method Newsletter*, after a few years, you might have more positions than you feel comfortable with. In this case, I recommend that you sell the stock in your portfolio that ranks the lowest in the complete ranking and use the proceeds to buy one of the Top10 stocks in which you own the least dollar amount. (If you are close to retirement, you may decide to sell the lowest-ranking stock and buy one of the Top10 stocks instead or, depending on your situation, you may not even reinvest the proceeds in equities at that stage.)

The process of portfolio building is really easy once you start investing and get in the swing of it. **And don't forget: if you have questions, I am always here to help the members of the FALCON family.**

RECAP

Dissecting the "Black Box Model"

Although the FALCON Method truly encompasses all the money pipes of corporate operations (as detailed in the "black box" section), some of the connections between our model's components and the pipes themselves may not be obvious at first. This is why I decided to provide a really short summary of the most important issues below.

A company's value stems from the "no-strings-attached cash" it can generate, the so-called free cash flow. The FALCON Method focuses on firms where this free cash flow has made an immaculate dividend history of at least 20 years possible. As a first step, our selection of the "Premium Dividend Club" stocks addresses the crucial role of free cash flow (no company without consistent earnings power and cash making capacity can give two decades of stable or increasing dividends to its shareholders).To make things even more explicit, the FALCON Method also examines the free cash flow yield as an absolute threshold criterion. What's the connection with the money pipes? The free cash flow category itself covers the following pipes: **revenues, ongoing expenses, taxes, and capital expenditures**.

You can see stock transactions on both the input and output sides of the black box model. As investors, we hate when the company issues stock and dilutes our ownership stake, but we certainly like it when they buy back their (undervalued) stock. The shareholder yield component of the FALCON Method addresses stock issuances and buybacks, so it helps us uncover the dirty tricks some managers employ to deceive their shareholders. Related pipes are **equity sale and share buyback**.

The question of leverage gets tackled by the three component shareholder yield (which contains the debt paydown) and the examination of the return on invested capital (ROIC), which must be way above the interest on debt. Related pipes are **borrowed money and payments on debts**.

The ROIC also helps us uncover how well the management deploys the retained earnings. Related pipe: **retained earnings**.

I'm sure that the "dividends" pipe does not need further explanation, but you may have noticed that the output pipe called "acquisitions of other companies" was nowhere to be found above. This particular pipe is not addressed directly in the FALCON Method because acquisitions are simply an external growth method, and what we are really interested in is the result of the transaction (that is, its effect on free cash flow and dividend). In general, I am not a fan of acquisitions, as they are riskier than reinvesting in the organic growth of the company, but the top managers behind such immaculate dividend histories tend to know what they are doing.

It is almost impossible to judge an acquisition in advance, even if you read all the available information on the announced transaction, so it is much better to focus on its long-term effects. By keeping a close eye on dividends, free cash flow, and ROIC, you are basically demanding that management put the company's money (that is, your money, since you are a part-owner) to the best possible use so that the firm's cash-generating capacity can increase and your dividends can grow along with it.

For the sake of conciseness, this explanation might be oversimplified at some points, but this section has one single goal, and that is to remind you that **the FALCON Method examines the companies** from various angles and only gives the green light when all three dimensions (operations, capital allocation, and valuation) are right. No important detail can hide from the eyes of the falcon.

Let me emphasize again, however, that the FALCON Method is 90% based on quantitative factors and certainly does not involve reading all the corporate filings with their sometimes very revealing footnotes. I leave this kind of tedious work to Buffett and his handful of followers; instead the FALCON Method identifies the companies that are operated well, have consistent earnings power, treat shareholders as partners, pay increasing dividends, buy back their shares, and have attractive stock valuations. When all these factors point in the right direction, outperformance is virtually guaranteed on a portfolio level. (You can run into one or two bad apples, but the rest of your portfolio will more than compensate for them.)

> *"So the really big money tends to be made by investors who are right on qualitative decisions—but, at least in my opinion, the more sure money tends to be made on the obvious quantitative decisions."*
> ~ Warren Buffett, 1967

Even Warren Buffett admits that the surest way to make money is to stick with the obvious quantitative decisions like the FALCON Method does. The alternative is to become a full-time qualitative investor and devote your life to this.

> *"I read and read and read. I probably read five to six hours a day."*
> ~ Warren Buffett

It is one thing to agree with most of Buffett's investment principles, but it is a completely different thing to try and copy his style without putting in the same amount of work he does. Chances are that no matter how much you read, you will not be able to mimic the Oracle of Omaha and judge the long-term competitiveness of businesses with such a high confidence that you can manage a highly concentrated portfolio of stocks based on your conviction. Instead of that demanding and stressful approach, most of us should go with the "more sure money" theory and live a meaningful life alongside investing in a sensible way.

AFTERWORD

The Key to Success You Hold

"If you can't describe what you are doing as a process, you don't know what you're doing. We should work on our process, not the outcome of our processes."

~ W. Edwards Deming[70]

The FALCON Method is an all-around investment process that is made up of proven elements. This, however, does not mean that all the stocks you purchase based on the newsletter will be big winners from the moment you press the "buy" button. You need to understand that intelligent investing is probabilistic and not deterministic, which means that by consistently executing a strategy that tilts the odds of outperformance in your favor, you will achieve superior results in the long run...but you will have to accept the inevitability of errors along the way. Simply put: you will surely have losers in your portfolio, but the winners will more than compensate for them.

All you can do is focus on the process and its consistent execution, no matter how you feel. It is easier said than done, but this is exactly what sensible investing is about. There are similarities between investing wisely and playing a poker hand well. Just have a look at the "process versus outcome" matrix of Russo and Schoemaker before we proceed:

Good Process

Good Outcome – deserved success

Bad Outcome – bad break

Bad Process

Good Outcome – dumb luck

Bad Outcome – poetic justice

You can play a poker hand terribly (like going all-in pre-flop with your off-suit 7 and 2) and still win it[71]. This is because the outcome of a single hand is strongly influenced by randomness, or luck if you like. But continue to do this kind of silly stuff at the poker table and you are sure to go broke. With a bad process, the odds are against you, and the more you play, the higher your probability of losing grows. With your first hand, you could have dumb luck (the combination of a bad process and good outcome), but later you will face poetic justice (the combination of bad process and a deserved bad outcome).

The opposite is also true, though, and **this makes investing a psychological rather than an intellectual endeavor**: you can excel at the disciplined execution of a good process that tilts the odds of winning in your favor (like the FALCON Method), but you will still run into some bad breaks. Some of your stock selections will not work out, which is like losing a poker hand with your pair of aces; it can happen, but you must not let it throw you off the right track. You absolutely *must* continue to play the game wisely; stick to your good process and the deserved success will come.

Why am I throwing this stuff in here instead of just finishing this book and selling my newsletter? Because I am honest and want to highlight the real key to your success, which is *you*. Mark Hulbert[72] has been independently tracking the performance of several investment newsletters for decades and notes that most of the time, subscribers to the newsletters achieve subpar performance compared to the newsletter they follow. The reason is simple: most subscribers fail to act consistently. (Notice that I am not talking about the quality of the processes the underlying newsletters employ, but rather the way the subscribers use the recommendations they get. Even if the newsletter is a decent one—which is a big "if"—most people fail to reap the rewards of their subscription.)

No matter how good the FALCON Method is—and I certainly hope you're convinced about its quality by now—consistency on your part is essential to your success.

> *"The main point is to have the right general principles and the character to stick to them."*
> ~ Benjamin Graham[73]

I have filled dozens of pages to show you the general principles behind the FALCON Method. Now it is your turn to make a decision about whether this approach is something you feel comfortable with. You can only stick with it through thick and thin if you understand the process and accept it wholeheartedly. Consistency is vital for a good performance—just remember the example of why the S&P 500 index is hard to beat!

With the *FALCON Method Newsletter*, the first key to your success (having a good process) is firmly in place: all the factors involved point toward outperformance. The second key (your consistent execution) has gotten a huge boost by focusing on reputable, quality dividend payers that give you more and more passive income, no matter how their stock prices might fluctuate. These are well-known stocks that are easy to buy and hold. The psychology of investing cannot get much more manageable than this, so I wholeheartedly hope that the members of the FALCON family will enjoy great success.

See you on board!

Book Discounts and Special Deals

About the Author

*"Being honest may not get you a lot of friends, but it will
always get you the right ones."*
~ John Lennon[74]

I was born in Hungary in 1982. My parents got divorced before I
turned 10 and this had a huge influence on my life. I stayed with
my mother, who was working as a kindergarten teacher, while my
father became one of the most successful businessmen in our town. I

saw two very different financial realities at a young age and made a decision that determined my path: I wanted to become financially free as quickly as possible so that I would not need to put in long hours (like my father, who was always working) to get the kind of income that let me go to the grocery store and shop with the feeling that I could afford to buy anything I desire (which we most certainly could not do on my mother's salary).

This motivation led me to become an economist and start my career as an equity analyst at Hungary's most reputable online financial journal. Because I wanted to break free, I established and sold my first company by the age of 24, and more of the same "building and selling" processes followed afterwards. I benefited immensely from having built companies from scratch, seeing the black box model in operation. This is an advantage many investors do not have.

> *"I am a better investor because I am a businessman, and a better businessman because I am an investor."*
>
> ~ Warren Buffett

Having been the CEO of companies in different fields (e-commerce, digital agency, media, etc.), I can honestly tell you that as an outside investor, you have absolutely no chance to see what is happening inside the black box. You will never know the tiny details, so it is better to accept this and focus on the money-carrying input and output pipes connected to the black box—those are the ones that are really important and are still visible from the outside. Having lived both sides of the story—the CEO and the investor roles—I am sure that superior investment results can be achieved by focusing on the money pipes just as the FALCON Method does.

Since investing is my passion, I surrendered all my executive roles at the age of 33 (I kept some ownership stake in one of my companies but retired from its operative management) and became a full-time investor. I have read hundreds of books along the way and asked the authors and other reputable investors tons of questions until my investment process began to crystallize. I wrote a book on dividend investing that became a category bestseller in Hungary and taught my approach in both personal and online video formats. I have done all this teaching and writing without a definite financial motivation (since I was already living off passive income at that stage). My goal was to get my message to as many people as possible and help them move in the right direction.

As mentioned before, I got an invitation to speak at a financial conference in 2016, where people from the audience flocked to me after the presentation and were so enthusiastic that they kept asking questions for more than an hour (during our lunch break). The only question I could not answer back then sounded like this: "Couldn't you just share with us the list of stocks you think present the best investment opportunities? Not everyone would like to put in the same amount of work you did, but this process really looks well-built and logical, so we would use its results if we could."

This is how the *FALCON Method Newsletter* was born. Up until its launch, I was driving full throttle with my eyes closed, putting in an enormous effort to teach my way of investing to as many people as possible, but I failed to realize that most of them only wanted to understand the underlying thought process; once they were convinced that my approach should work, they wanted me to manage their money, or at least help them with stock selection. The newsletter service is as close to this desired solution as possible, and it is more than affordable to most of the people who trust the process I have outlined in this book. I wrote all these pages so that you wouldn't have to buy a pig in a poke as with most newsletters. Please take your time, understand how the FALCON Method works, and once you think that you can consistently follow this investment system in the long run, I welcome you on board.

In closing, let me share with you a part of a song I used to listen to often while training for my first Ironman triathlon race. It sums up nicely how I think about life and goal-setting, and how I managed to achieve everything I've done so far. I wish you all the best and hope to see you in the FALCON family.

Maybe there's another path that'll

Get you there a little bit faster

But I'm sticking with the one inside of me

That's the only way I know

Don't stop 'til everything's gone

Straight ahead, never turn round

Don't back up, don't back down

Full throttle, wide open

You get tired and you don't show it

Dig a little deeper when you think you can't dig no more

That's the only way I know.

(Lyrics of "The Only Way I Know" by Jason Aldean)

The *FALCON Method Newsletter* helps you to take advantage of the systematic mistakes that most humans make, rather than suffer from them. It gets you to buy top-quality stocks when they are marked down because of psychological biases. The most important thing is to buy quality on sale and to do this consistently and systematically, while measuring the results of your entire investment portfolio and not focusing on only a few of your individual stocks. You have complete control over the process and the results will take care of themselves in the long run. By buying a diversified portfolio based on just the numbers, not emotions, you have taken your first step toward financial freedom.

Get your special discount on the *FALCON Method Newsletter* with this coupon:

READITALL30

Use it here:

https://thefalconmethod.com/newsletter-30day-special

Remember, you have a 30-day free trial and you will be shielded from all future price hikes; your annual subscription fee stays $97 as long as you are on board.

Endnotes

1 https://www.bloomberg.com/news/videos/2016-11-04/the-david-rubenstein-show-warren-buffett

2 http://www.berkshirehathaway.com/letters/2011ltr.pdf

3 If you have doubts, read the story of one of the world's most renowned economists, John Maynard Keynes, who was a hopeless speculator and market timer before converting to value investing. (See: *Concentrated Investing* by Benello, Van Biema, &Carlisle)

4 Again, if you have your doubts, please check out this US inflation calculator that measures the buying power of the dollar over time using the official US government data: http://www.usinflationcalculator.com. The US dollar has lost 95% of its purchasing power between 1913 (the creation of the Fed) and 2013 according to U.S. Bureau of Labor Statistics (http://z822j1x8tde3wuovlgo7ue15.wpengine.netdna-cdn.com/wp-content/uploads/2014/08/USD_PP1.png).

5 https://en.wikipedia.org/wiki/Jeremy_Siegel

6 https://robertgallen.com/about-robert-g-allen

7 https://en.wikipedia.org/wiki/John_Maynard_Keynes

8 https://en.wikipedia.org/wiki/Peter_Lynch

9 Fred Schwed's fantastic book *Where Are the Customers' Yachts*? is a classic on this topic.

10 Chapter C-7, p. 118-120.

11 http://www.berkshirehathaway.com/letters/1981.html

12 Earnings figures in the company's Profit and Loss Statement (P&L) are not the same as the "surplus cash" I am referring to. Profit and cash flow numbers can differ considerably, and by the end of this book, you will know exactly which figures to focus on.

13 http://www.berkshirehathaway.com/letters/2010ltr.pdf

14 https://en.wikipedia.org/wiki/Benjamin_Graham

15 In my opinion, the best books on quantitative investing are: *What Works on Wall Street* by James O'Shaughnessy, *Quantitative Value* by Wesley Gray and Tobias E. Carlisle, and *The Little Book that Still Beats the Market* by Joel Greenblatt.

16 https://en.wikipedia.org/wiki/Joel_Greenblatt

17 https://en.wikipedia.org/wiki/John_D._Rockefeller

18 https://en.wikipedia.org/wiki/David_Dreman

19 https://en.wikipedia.org/wiki/Yogi_Berra

20 A tiny company.

21 https://www.linkedin.com/in/alangotthardt/

22 https://en.wikipedia.org/wiki/Jeremy_Siegel

23 https://en.wikipedia.org/wiki/Jeremy_Siegel

24 You can find it here: http://us.spindices.com/indices/strategy/sp-500-dividend-aristocrats

25 http://www.dripinvesting.org/tools/tools.asp

26 A company that has been paying higher and higher dividends for at least 25 consecutive years is called a Dividend Champion.

27 By no means do I want to make you think that Boeing paid more dividends in this period than Mercury General did. Instead, the example serves to highlight that investing in a "Dividend Champion" does not automatically mean seeing massively growing dividends.

28 https://en.wikipedia.org/wiki/Jeremy_Siegel

29 $100 divided by 100 shares

30 $259 divided by 100 shares

31 https://en.wikipedia.org/wiki/Joel_Greenblatt

32 Price return alone, not counting the dividends you could get along the way.

33 Okay, I will. If you sell out the same share you bought at 8 times earnings at a multiple of 15 (which is still too conservative to describe a situation of euphoria), then your return skyrockets to 386%.

34 http://www.berkshirehathaway.com/letters/1991.html

35 The actual earnings per share figure is multiplied by 15 every year.

36 https://www.oaktreecapital.com/people/bio/howard-marks

37 Notice that we haven't sold at the overvalued levels, because I wanted to show you an example of unchanged multiples. By the way, no one can guarantee that the stock you purchase will ever become overvalued, so there is no use speculating on that. Buy top quality on the cheap and your job is done! Time will take care of the rest.

38 https://en.wikipedia.org/wiki/Walter_Schloss

39 If, for some reason, you do not find the differences in annual returns meaningful, have a look at the following calculation of what even a 1 percentage point difference in annual return can mean in the long run. Investing $1,000 for 20 years at an annual rate of 10% gives you $6,728 by the end of the period, while this result could grow to $8,062 with a slight increase in the annual rate of return to 11%.

40 I will define this free cash flow category in a moment.

41 https://en.wikipedia.org/wiki/Peter_Lynch

42 Calculating with a forward annual dividend of $3 and a stock price of $100, the dividend yield is 3% (3/100).

43 This is calculated by deducting capital expenditures (called capex) from the operating cash flow. (A better approach is to split the capital expenditures to maintenance and growth components and deduct only the maintenance capex that is to keep the company at the same level. Unfortunately, this is easier said than done, so most investors simply deduct the full capex.)

44 http://www.berkshirehathaway.com/letters/1980.html

45 The free cash flow yield is calculated in the following way: free cash flow per share / share price.

46 The shareholder yield is the sum of the dividend yield and the buyback yield, where the buyback yield measures how much a company has bought back its shares in the last 12 months over a company's market capitalization.

47 http://www.berkshirehathaway.com/letters/2014ltr.pdf

48 Byron Wien and Frances Lim, "Lessons from Buyback and Dividend Announcements," October 4, 2004.

49 The book *What Works on Wall Street* by James O'Shaughnessy can provide enough evidence all on its own.

50 The FALCON Method prefers the shareholder yield indicator that includes the net-debt paydown component, since it is a good way to filter out companies that are financing the major part of their shareholder returns by taking on debt. If such an indicator is not available, the FALCON Method provides another criterion to address the issue of debt.

51 The data is accurate as of the time of writing (20 January, 2017).

52 The two-component version that includes dividends and buybacks.

53 The yield on your original investment would still be 2.85% at the end of the 10th year, even if you reinvested all the dividends you received along the way.

54 A 10% growth rate would catapult your yield on cost to 5.55% by the end of the 10th year. I hope you notice the difference. (And the stock price should have increased along with the dynamic growth as well.)

55 https://sugar.mhinvest.com/highcharts/investment.php

56 The figures I picked for the sake of illustration are Chowder-like numbers, so they are the sum of the current dividend yield and the dividend growth rate of certain timeframes.

57 As of January 2017, Mercury did survive the competition, but in this weighted multifactor ranking process, it only collected 35.37 points of the possible 100, which means it was ranked 285th of the 325 stocks evaluated.

58 Stocks offering a potential double-dip benefit are easy to identify, and so are the ones with extra-high valuation multiples, but human judgment must be employed with those somewhere in the middle.

59 As of early 2017, Coke's free cash flow yield and dividend yield were almost equal, which means that the company pays out nearly all the cash it generates. This illustrates how dividend coverage came into the picture (indirectly) long before the final phase of the FALCON Method.

60 The DPS/FCF ratio was 96% as of January 2017.

61 Net Income / (Total Equity + Long-Term Debt)

62 This again is pointed out in James O'Shaughnessy's book *What Works on Wall Street*.

63 http://www.stockopedia.com/content/glenn-greenberg-the-best-value-investor-youve-never-heard-of-88234/

64 https://en.wikipedia.org/wiki/Benjamin_Graham

65 https://en.wikipedia.org/wiki/Benjamin_Franklin

66 http://www.berkshirehathaway.com/letters/1996.html

67 https://en.wikipedia.org/wiki/Paul_Samuelson

68 https://en.wikipedia.org/wiki/Peter_Lynch

69 In their book *Investment Analysis and Portfolio Management*, Frank Reilly and Keith Brown reported that in one set of studies for randomly selected stocks, "...about 90% of the maximum benefit of diversification was derived from portfolios of 12 to 18 stocks." In other words, if you own about 12 to 18 stocks, you have obtained more than 90% of the benefits of diversification, assuming you own an equally weighted portfolio.

70 https://en.wikipedia.org/wiki/W._Edwards_Deming

71 This example refers to a hand of Texas Hold'em Poker, where 7-2 off-suit (meaning the cards are of different suits) is considered one of the worst starting hands. Even if you do not know the rules of the game, it is pretty easy to accept that you shouldn't risk all your money (go all-in) on one of the worst starting hands you could possibly get.

72 http://hulbertratings.com/

73 http://hulbertratings.com/

74 https://en.wikipedia.org/wiki/John_Lennon

Lightning Source UK Ltd.
Milton Keynes UK
UKHW022032011020
370871UK00005B/296

9 781631 610400